Main Economic Policy Areas of the EEC

edited by

PETER COFFEY

Europa Institute
University of Amsterdam
Amsterdam, The Netherlands

1983

SPRINGER-SCIENCE+BUSINESS MEDIA, B.V.

Library of Congress Cataloging in Publication Data CIP

Main entry under title:

Main economic policy areas of the EEC.

Includes index.
1. European Economic Community countries--Economic policy. 2. European Economic Community countries--Commercial policy. 3. Agriculture and state--European Economic Community countries. 4. Industry and state--European Economic Community countries. 5. Fiscal policy--European Economic Country countries. 6. Regional planning--European Economic Community countries. 7. Monetary policy--European Economic Community countries. I. Coffey, Peter.
HC241.2.M2374 1983 338.94 82-22484

ISBN 978-94-017-2132-5 ISBN 978-94-017-2130-1 (eBook)
DOI 10.1007/978-94-017-2130-1

Table of Contents

INTRODUCTION

by Peter Coffey

This is indeed a most opportune time for the publication of a serious, critical and independent study about the "Main Economic Policy Areas of the EEC".

The European Economic Community is the world's most important commercial and trading bloc and its economic policies consequently have the most far-reaching implications for all countries in the world. The rest of the world is acutely conscious of the Community's trading policies. In turn, these policies (apart from those based on historical links - antecedent to the EEC's formation) are strongly influenced by the internal economic policies of the Common Market - especially by the Common Agricultural Policy (CAP).

At the present time, the Community finds itself, both internally and externally, at a crossroads. This crossroads takes the form of a choice between 'protectionism' or 'openness'. Unfortunately, present evidence suggests that currently and in the immediately foreseeable future the former option has been chosen by the EEC.

This move in the direction of 'protectionism' places independent experts before the responsibility of examining critically the Community's main economic policy areas and of making proposals for future policy options. The editor therefore decided to invite a number of distinguished colleagues who are regular lecturers on the International Postgraduate Course in European Integration at the Europa Instituut in the University of Amsterdam to examine the EEC's most important economic policy areas. In selecting these policy areas, it was decided to include only the most important classical ones where, on the whole, constant progress - closely linked to integration in the Common Market - has been observed over a relatively long period of time.

The contributors have examined the chosen policy areas both from a theoretical, as well as from a practical or applied angle. The record of these policy areas is assessed and proposals are made for future policy changes. Readers will thus have the possibility of using these proposals as a point of reference when, during the course of the coming year, they themselves come to judge the evolution of the main economic policies of the EEC.

The European Economic Community thus finds itself at perhaps the most critical crossroads in its history. It is the editor's hope that this book, the work of independent experts, will have a constructive influence on those who take important decisions regarding the choice and application of policies in the Common Market.

Amsterdam, September 1982

Acknowledgements

Apart from wishing to thank his colleagues who have contributed to this work in such a friendly and co-operative manner, the editor also wishes to thank Mme. Laura Schiesswald and Mr. B. Kotmans of the Secretariat of the Europa Instituut for their assistance in typing major parts of the manuscript of this work.

Likewise, thanks are due to Mr. H. Baarh, a student at the Europa Instituut, who has prepared the index for this book.

Notes about the contributors

Peter Coffey is Head of the Economics Section at the Europa Instituut, University of Amsterdam. He has published many works on European and international economic and monetary problems. Mr. Coffey, who speaks seven languages, has lectured in most countries of the EEC, as well as in many other parts of the world.

Alexis P. Jacquemin is Professor of Economics at the Institute of Economics at the University of Louvain. An expert on industrial and competition policy, he has lectured and published widely in Europe and North America.

Willem Molle is Head of the Division Industrial and Location Studies at the Netherlands Economic Institute, Rotterdam, and Professor at the University of Limburg in Maastricht. He has been for many years responsible for research on behalf of the EEC Regional Policy Directorate-General, and has published several works about regional and industrial questions.

Piet van den Noort is Professor of Agricultural Economics in the Department of Agricultural Economics at the Agricultural University of Wageningen. He has published many works about the EEC's Common Agricultural Policy.

Alan R. Prest is Professor of Economics in the Economics Department of the London School of Economics. He is an acknowledged international authority on fiscal questions and has advised national and international authorities about fiscal matters. Professor Prest has lectured in all parts of the world and has published several major classic works on fiscal issues.

PART ONE

THE COMMON AGRICULTURAL POLICY KEY TO EUROPEAN ECONOMIC INTEGRATION

by

P.C. van den Noort

1 THE ECONOMIC BACKGROUND: LACK OF ELASTICITY, SOLIDARITY AND AUTHORITY

On closely examining the workings of the economy some are surprised to find a pervading natural order, whilst others are most struck by precisely the chaotic nature of activity. These two positions correspond to the two views of society as in harmony or as in conflict. The belief in a harmonious natural order in the economy evolved largely as a result of the discovery of the circular flow of goods and income by the first economists in 18th century France. They were of the opinion that the order, rather than originating from supranatural powers or worldly authorities, was brought about by the interaction of all the producers and consumers in the market. The price mechanism had been discovered as the anonymous regulator of the economy.
Infact it was the means by which a state of equilibrium could be achieved in which:

- Exactly the quantity of everything desired by consumers is produced.
- Welfare is maximized, for the given circumstances.
- Welfare is distributed in a reasonable manner.

That all this is possible in the market economy forms one of the most important tenets of Neo-classical economics and is often referred to as Pareto's Theorem of Optimality. It is the pet idea of economic textbooks and the stumbling block of those who visualise a Conflict-model.
The position of Agriculture in the circular flow was given special attention right from the beginning. The Physiocrats saw (if erroneously) Agriculture itself as the motor of the economic process. A view which one still comes across today.
The Physiocrats and many other economists of the day can be seen as practical moralists. A prescription for the improvement of economic welfare was always tacked onto the end of their analyses. At the time France was

Coffey, P. (ed.): Main Economic Policy Areas of the EEC
©1983. Martinus Nijhoff Publishers, The Hague / Boston / London
ISBN 90-247-2793-6.

struggling along in a state of stagnation and precarious food self-sufficiency. The authorities were aware of the necessity of firmly regulating the economy and production and trade were strictly controlled. The Physiocrats were however of the opinion that this action was only increasing the problems. They thought that production and trade should be liberalised; 'Laissez faire, Laissez passer' became their slogan. This idea gained more and more support as the 18th and 19th centuries progressed. As a result European Agriculture became more and more a part of an expanding market economy. Agriculture is assigned a special place in such a system and has several characteristic attributes; I will mention a number of them here and try to show their practical relevance.

First I shall concentrate on some of the characteristics of Demand for Agricultural products. The so-called price elasticity seems to vary between -0.1 and -0.4, and the income elasticity between 0.1 and 0.3. The richer the country the lower are these elasticities. Dry facts but with unexpectedly far reaching implications for society.

Low price elasticity means that the unavoidable variation in production of about 5% a year causes price variations on a much larger scale. Thus both food producers and consumers must contend with highly fluctuating prices and thus fluctuating incomes.

The low income elasticity of demand for agricultural products means that in an expanding economy only a small part of the extra income is spent on extra food. Thus agricultural products form a relatively smaller part of total consumption. The result is that agriculture becomes a relatively declining sector: see fig. 1.

As far as supply is concerned, the price elasticity is low in both the short and the long term, but it is positive. There is no question of a negative supply reaction (i.e. higher output as price falls) for agriculture as a whole. This contrasts with popular belief. The low positive price elasticity of Supply means that when demand falls (in a recession or a depression) farmers continue producing more or less the same quantities, even though their incomes fall as prices drop. This phenomenon is very different from the production patterns of industrial products, where quantities can be more easily adjusted and the reduction in price is thus less severe: see fig. 2. In addition and in contrast to earlier postulations Supply seems able to expand greatly and at a rate not much less than that of Industry.

This expansion however runs up against the little expanding inelastic demand. In the past when this occurred it resulted in downward pressure on agricultural prices and the relative decline of agriculture (and thus the declining importance of rural areas) was reinforced. Structural change of great proportions occured. The stimulation of productivity which should have been in the farmers' favour, improving their income position and living conditions, infact resulted in lower prices, thus putting pressure on income levels, and caused migration to other occupations, often in the town. These phenomena follow logically from the above mentioned characteristics of the market for agricultural products, although this is not often recognised. The unexpected result is assigned to the dark powers of Capitalism.

The market is not transparent and no-one knows what the price level will be at any point in the future. Many have been enticed into growing according to ruling market conditions because of this, this leads to cyclic price fluctuations; the pig cycle for example is well known.
Technical change made it possible and worthwhile processing agricultural products in factories. As time has passed farmers have sold a smaller and smaller part of their produce directly, to consumers. Sale is left up to trade and industry. Big companies have developed, joined together and formed multi-nationals. Market form has changed from being the much praised atomistic market to one with oligopolistic tendencies. The bargaining position of the individual farmer has been weakened.

Finally I would like to mention some products, like 'farmyard stench' and 'countryside', which classical theory has more or less ignored. These things reach the consumer outside the market framework, they influence the level of welfare but cannot be regulated by the market mechanism.
One must note with regard to positive external effects, such as produced by beautiful countryside for example, that whilst it is "valued" highly in the free market economy the consumer neither pays for it nor does the producer receive anything.
Modern production methods sometimes necessitate the farmer altering (i.e. spoiling) the countryside, much to the displeasure of the town dwellers who use the countryside for recreational purposes. The price mechanism cannot resolve this matter, the market leaves it uncontested.

Fig. 1

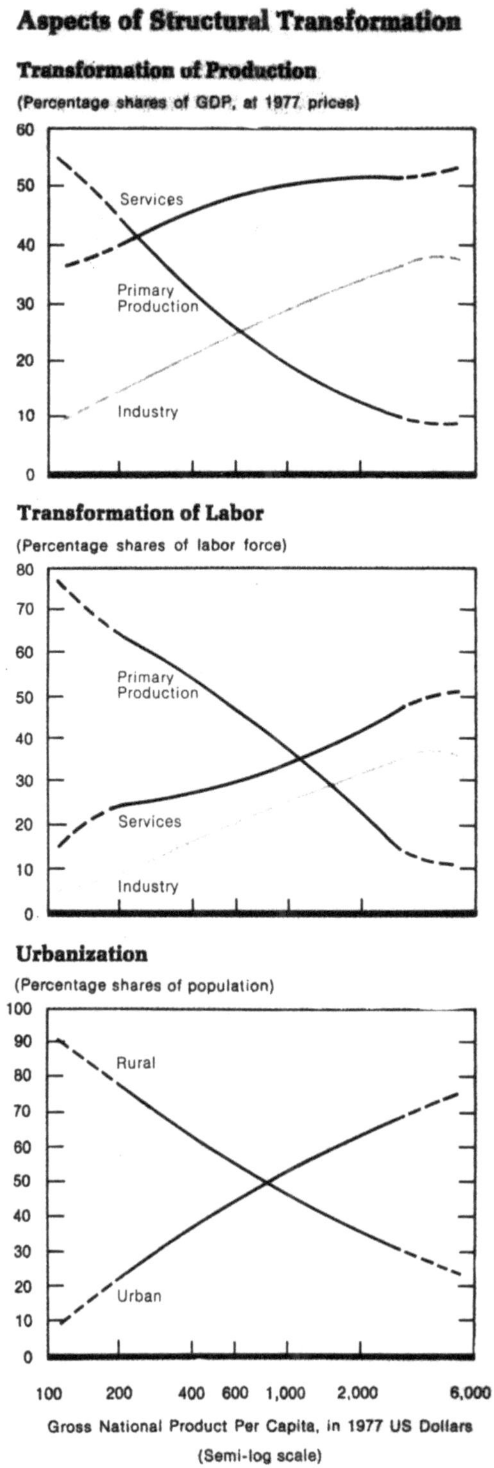

Source:
The World Bank

Fig. 2

World indices of production and trade (1929=100)

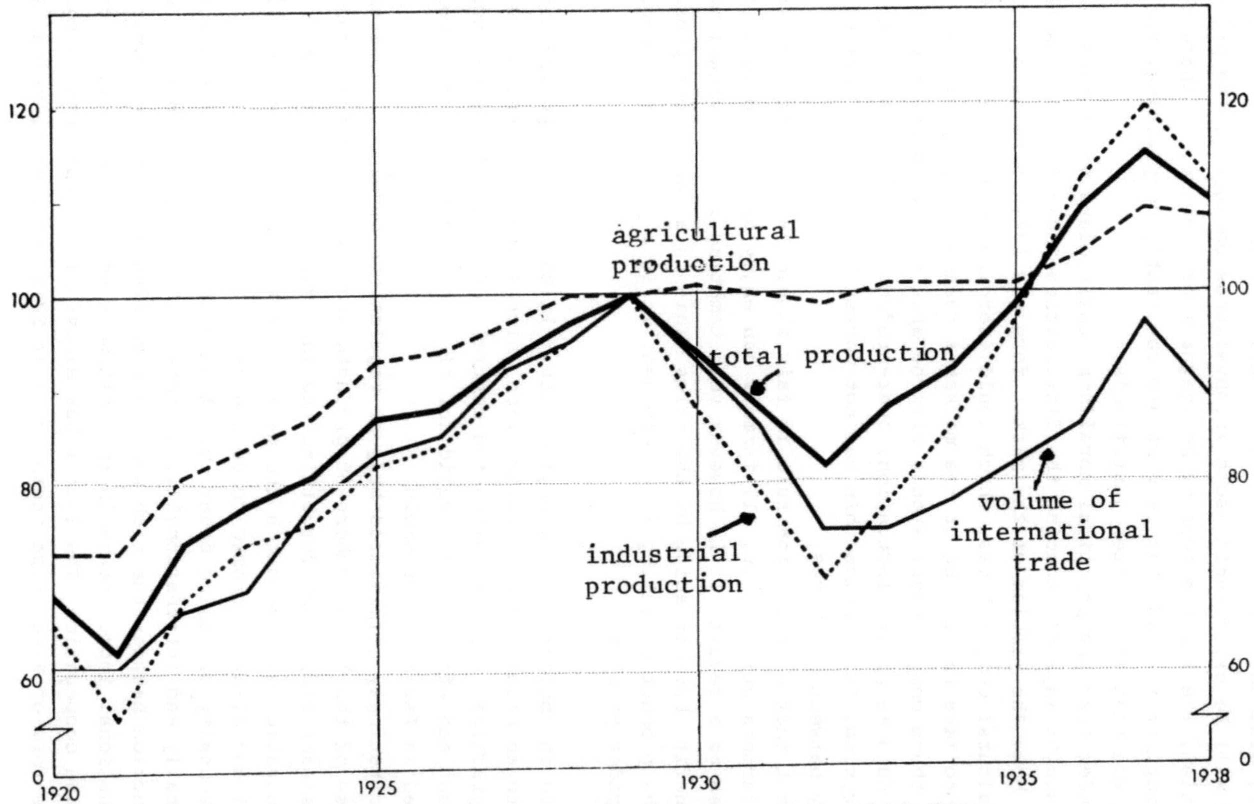

Source: Het internationale economische leven, 1913-1946;CBS,
Monographie van de Nederlandse conjunctuur no. 6, 1947

One may draw the conclusion that at anytime either the farmer or the consumer will be experiencing some inconvenience because of the price mechanism, whether the economy be stagnant or growing, or there be boom or slump. It is said that farmers are constantly complaining, but one might add that it is often justifiable.
No wonder that the practical moralists, politicians and interested parties sought ways of reducing the difficulties indicated. Let us now consider how. The problem of the market form was taken care of by setting up agricultural cooperatives, which could exercise countervailing power in order to make bargaining on the market a reasonable proposition. In principle these cooperatives should also be able to act in other problem areas such as price fluctuation, over-production and the spoiling of the countryside. In practice this has not worked because of a lack of solidarity between producers.
The fact that a production rule is fair should be sufficient to ensure that farmers stick to it. All farmers can enjoy higher and more stable incomes as a result. It is however very tempting for individual members to benefit, but not abide by the rules. This is a contagious process and the production ruling is undermined. It is a form of the so-called 'freerider problem'.

Despite the beliefs of the Physiocrats, 'laissez faire' policy can thus lead to an undesirable situation from which state intervention is the only practical way out, since the central body can enforce rulings which are just and effective and valid for all, and the free-rider problem is reduced as far as is possible.
An irritatingly complicated body of regulations developed, however, because of the large numbers of products and the wide differences within the peasant class, not forgetting the many different countries: i.e. a bureaucratic chaos to match the market chaos with sometimes very detrimental social and economic consequences.
The necessity of making order out of this chaos was soon seen, both nationally and internationally. At this point it is pertinant to make a distinction between the rich western countries and the non-western poor. International improvements in the west were possible because of consultation and cooperation. The latter has evolved in Europe into integration in the form of Free trade areas (such as EFTA) or Customs unions (such

as the EEC). This has meant that it has been possible to streamline regulations or even make them identical. Within such a union more order and harmony may be created, but the result is not seldom further divorce from the world market.
Thus it is also desirable to improve the functioning of international markets by entering into commodity agreements. Exporting and importing countries can come together and stabilize the prices, production and consumption of important products. Many attempts have been made, but the results have been negligible. This is because of wide differences in interests, mistrust and lack of international solidarity; in other words, the free-rider problem on a world scale and the lack of supra-national authority to counter it.
Action has not been limited to these commodity agreements: a development policy toward poorer countries has also been seen as necessary: free trade, development assistance, special provisions in international agreements etc. Philosophy and practice were changed in the post 1945 period. If the preoccupation at first was with free trade and industrialisation then this underwent a noticiable change following e.g. the publication of the FAO World agriculture plan in 1969, the rise of the green revolution and the conclusions of the studies carried out for the Club of Rome. Rural development was more frequently given high priority.
Whilst agriculture developed very quickly in western nations, change in the poorer countries has only occured at a moderate pace. The world market has not been revitalised or made to function better. Rather disorder on a world scale has resulted.

At the regional and national levels as well as in the context of the problems at the world level, which I have touched upon, one hears the lament: 'Why don't economists calculate exactly what must be done?'
The answer is that they are not capable of it.
This is not only because it is difficult to formulate adequate models, since there is insufficient data on the relationships within an economy and the future is unknown, but also (and this is often forgotten) because it is not clear 'what we want' and 'what is good for us'. Or put more formally the functional objectives of economic policy are unknown. Thus, the social welfare function is postulated in many theories of economic policy but is in fact unknown. The social welfare function is the biggest

fiction of the textbooks. So it is an illusion to think that in reality the optimal policy can be calculated by maximising the social welfare function in an economic model. In fact, politicians must arrive at decisions on limited information. In the various western countries traditions have been built up as to how to arrive at political decisions, also without thorough investigations by economists; however, the more heterogeneous the group aimed at and the greater the number of participating states the more difficult it is to reach decisions. The ways in which the politicians find their decisions should be studied more by economists.

2 THE POLITICAL BACKGROUND: 'THE GREAT GRAIN DEAL'

Agriculture has a special and prominent position in the process of European Integration. It sometimes seems as if the policy eminating from Brussels is primarily directed towards fulfilling the needs of agriculture. This is clearly an incorrect picture. The most important motivation behind post war European Integration was the desire to achieve enduring peace and long term security in Europe and thus prevent extremism, revenge and retaliation or revolution.
To do this it was essential to ensure peace and friendship between France and Germany. One way of promoting this was through economic integration as was already taking place in the framework of the European Coal and Steel Community. The formation of a customs union for example would be an important step. This would imply among other things free trade in goods and common import regulations with respect to third countries. This in itself was attractive to Germany, even if agricultural goods were excluded, as in e.g. The European Free Trade Area (EFTA). This was not the case for France however since it was more competitive in the area of agricultural products, grains in particular. The 'deal' then was to include agriculture in such a way that France was sure of an profitable expansion of its grain exports in exchange for free trade in industrial goods. Such an expansion of exports could only result from certainty if there were a certain market and price policy i.e. France could only be sure of increased exports within the European Community if markets were open and the price level fixed at an agreeable target price-level. This target price had to be lower than the existing price level in Germany since it was intended that German production fall, grain consumption would increase and that France would supply the German consumer. This market for french grain would be further guaranteed by preferential treatment: Grain from third countries could only be imported at higher prices. It is this reasoning which underlies the policy that grain imported from third countries is charged a variable levy at point of entry.
It was agreed that target price level be determined by the desired price for the largest consumption area in Europe (Duisburg). The target price for other areas being derived from this by deducting the transactions and transport costs involved in getting it to Duisburg.

Even in periods when production in Europe was high and imports from overseas low the guaranteed price should not be allowed to fall too much, not more than about 7% under the (derived) target price. This to be achieved by compulsory purchase by a central body.
Grain is an input into the animal breeding and food-stuff industries. In order to maintain the competitive positions of these branches of industry on external markets a restitution equal to the import levy had to be paid on the grain component of these goods exported.
The outcome of the 'deal' was however only assured as long as there were sufficient funds available for intervention and restitutions. A European guarantee fund was set up with this in mind. It was supposed to be financed by the receipts of the import levies and be under common control. Measures which distorted competition were to be avoided.
Germany could not accept such a system just like that. There had to be provisions that the proposed policy would not result in a freezing of the structure of agriculture as it was: it had to be possible to adjust the size of agricultural employment and there should not be technical stagnation i.e. agricultural productivity had to continue to grow. Furthermore the reduction in guaranteed price (compared to the then existing national policy) must not result in farm incomes that were too low, but on the other hand consumers in Europe must not be saddled with prices that were too high.
It was in addition intended that the expansion of agricultural markets for France should not have too great an impact on the trade of traditional exporters. This is all laid down mainly in Article 39 of the Treaty of Rome. This article is concerned not so much with the formulation of the general goals of agricultural policy as is usually said but with the limiting conditions of the "deal".
The relatively efficient agricultural areas of France (and also the Netherlands) would profit from such a system, whilst for the inefficient areas the opposite would be the case. Thus European agricultural production would undergo a restructuralisation, which was referred to as regional specialisation. Regional specialisation is one of the well known concepts of International trade and the theory of Economic Integration. Dubbing the production effects of the grain deal the results of regional specialisation was to camouflage the special nature of the grain agreement.

The negotiating parties were not blind to the real motives and demanded concretisation of the limiting conditions. A long transition period (to 1970) was decided upon, to be made up of three stages each four years long, resulting (the gap being closed step-by-step) in a common price level. The German farmers were promised a direct, but temporary, supplementary payment to prevent what was seen as unreasonably large reductions in income. Even so, there was such great opposition that France had to use all the political pressure it could muster to get a binding agreement on the target price level for wheat. France made it impossible to cooperate on the accomodation of the external tariff for industrial products within the framework of the Kennedy Round until agreement had been reached regarding grain prices. This was a decisive argument. In 1964 a grain price arrangment was agreed upon which ratified the original deal with regard to grain. As from 1 July 1968 there was in fact a common market for soft wheat, the target price being 106 European Units of Account per ton.

There are certain substitution possibilities between this wheat and other products. By considering the marginal substitution relationships it is possible at the same time to determine the target prices of these other products. A market system was evolved to make these target prices also effective. Thus a common price policy for agriculture was arrived at and the customs union finally became a fact.

The expansion of the market for french grain envisaged by the deal was however, despite the detailed measures, not 100% guaranteed, since such a guarantee is dependent on the target price for wheat, and this was not yet determined for future years by an automatic mechanical procedure (a so-called objective method), it had to be fixed each year anew by a process of political bargaining.

Attempts were made up until recently to use a quasi-objective methodology in the price-fixing. The price increase should be equal to the increase of real costs on farms but there was no general consensus regarding the precise definition. In any case, the Council of Ministers usually fixed completely different percentage increases for the target price than the one calculated by this method. Presumably in order to keep within the bounds set by the 'limiting conditions', but perhaps also as a result of the constantly changing balance of power and opinion.

An agricultural price policy conducted by Brussels was something people had got used to during the transition period. When the customs union was finally realised some no longer saw the agricultural regulations as part of the 'deal' and as such a means of achieving integration, but as an agricultural policy in its own right. Some saw, for example, the prescriptions of Article 39 no longer as limiting conditions but as major goals of a European Agricultural policy and came with more optimal solutions for the European agricultural problems. Some of these plans proposed e.g. to adapt direct income payments instead of price policies. As to be expected, because of the political origins of the common agricultural policy, the market and price policy, being the core of the deal, were not in principal negotiable; Except for a few technical points such as the objective method, the price relationship between wheat and other products (e.g. the wheat'maize price ratio was much discussed), or the size of the grain component in export goods (such as eggs, pig meat). Only when integration was a long standing fact and the real nature of the 'deal' had been more or less forgotten and when difficulties within the policy became apparent was there any discussion about fundamentally modifying the CAP.
The latter difficulties were in fact inherent to the system itself.

3 COMPLICATIONS WITHIN THE SYSTEM

The Common Agricultural Policy is primarily a price policy, for a large number of products. Each product having its own system of market regulation and often its own terminology (see table 1), the prices being reviewed annually. These price adjustments have often been made at 'marathon sessions'. By subtracting the normal handling and transport charges to Duisburg from the target price the 'derived target price' for any other place can be obtained, on entry to the European Community (e.g. in Rotterdam) this is called the Threshold price. The difference between the world market price and the threshold price being bridged by a levy. On exporting grain or grain products a restitution of the levy being paid. Shipments of grain from America become more expensive during the crossing to Rotterdam. In Rotterdam the grain is sucked up into the "economic sluice" and its price raised to threshold level, then it is transported to the area of Europe with the greatest shortage and thus were the target price levels of Duisburg can be realised. If internal supply is relatively high then intervention is possible - for unlimited quantities. Neither is there any limitation on the quantity of grain or grain products for which restitution can be paid. The relationship between the target prices of the various grains is of crucial importance. The price ratio for wheat'maize was chosen in such a way that it was inevitable that wheat production would increase greatly. This, however, was in the interest of France.

Table 1 The EEC market regulation scheme

Arrangements / Commodities	Target price	Threshold price	Sluice gate price	Free at frontier price	Import levy	Supplementary levy	Import duty	Provision for market intervention	Provision for export refunds	Quota	Quality stadards	Producers Organisation	Initial date	Date for[10]) unification
Grain and grainproducts	□	□		□	□			□	□				1- 8-'62	1- 7-'67
Rice and riceproducts	□[1])	□		□	□			□[1])	□				1- 9-'64	1- 9-'67
Pigs and pigmeat			□		□	□		□	□				1- 8-'62	1- 7-'67
Poultry and eggs			□		□	□			□				1- 8-'62	1- 7-'67
Milk and dairyproducts	□[2])	□		□	□			□[9])	□					29- 7-'68
Beef and veal			□[3])	□	□		□	□	□	□[4])				29- 7-'68
Sugar and sugerbeets	□	□		□	□			□	□	□[5])			1- 7-'67	1- 7-'68
Oilseeds	□							□	□				1- 7-'67	1- 7-'67
Olive oil	□	□		□	□			□	□				1-11-'66	1-11-'66
Fruit and vegetables			□[6])	□		□	□	□	□	□[7])	□	□	1- 8-'62	1- 7-'68
Wine							□			□[8])	□		1- 8-'62	1-11-'69

[1]) In France and Italy
[2]) Only in case of milk
[3]) Guide price
[4]) Levy free import quotum for frozen beef
[5]) Production quotum
[6]) Reference price
[7]) Import quotum applicable only through a safe guard clause procedure
[8]) Import quotum
[9]) Applicable for butter and skimmed milkpowder
[10]) Since the dates mentioned the EEC is unified. This means a.o. that for the inner EEC-trade there are no import-levies any longer and furthermore that for the trade with third countries there are uniform import-levies and export-refunds.

The system of market regulation for grains was set out in great detail but one small point was overlooked, namely, the relationship with grain substitutes such as tapioca.
Tapioca was at the time an insignificant product on world markets and more expensive than grains, but as a result of the levies imported grains became dearer than tapioca. It was therefore a more attractive proposition to e.g. animal feed manufacturers, to use tapioca rather than grains. This meant that animal feed could be made more cheaply and intensive animal raising was given a stimulus. In addition, the restitution paid on the grain component of animal products was set somewhat high, which had the same effect as a subsidy. The degree to which stockrearing has expanded in the proximity of the ports is significant.

In the case of milk and dairy products, where the EEC is a net exporter (in contrast to the situation in grains), the same system is in fact operative. How can a higher internal price be achieved by using an import levy in the case of an export product? In fact it cannot be done. A subsidy is paid on dairy exports and this boosts the internal price. In order to prevent reimportation an import levy is instituted to match the export subsidy. The subsidy can now be better referred to as the restitution of that levy.
The Intervention mechanism of regulation also applies for dairy products – and again – for unlimited quantities. The only important product where there is a limit on the quantity for which Intervention is guaranteed is Sugar. If a farmer produces more than a certain quantity he no longer receives price support but only the world market price.
The price guarantee for unlimited quantities is one of the striking features of the Common Agricultural policy. In this sort of policy, if the price is set sbove the theoretical equilibrium level, the consumer consumes less (underconsumption) whilst the farmer produces more (overproduction). These are the two components of the Surplus.
This surplus is the consequence solely of the pricing policy. Growth of the surplus expresses itself in increases in the quantities offered to Intervention Boards and increases in the sums of money needed to finance it. Surplus production has diverse economic effects: as illustrated in table 2.

For Oil-seeds a levy is possible because of GATT regulations. This means that imports can take place at world market price. Protection takes on a different form. Exporters of European oil seeds receive a supplement or restitution equal to the size of the desired price support. This supplement is also paid to manufacturers for oil seeds grown in Europe, which have been processed. Which means that they are in a position to pay farmers the required price. The unlimited and untaxed quantities of imports of oil seed compete via margarine directly with butter and influence the price levels of animal feed concentrates, which affect the size of milk production.

Table 2 Some effects of the price guarantee system for the EEC as a whole

	Grains	Milk	Sugar
Consumer Surplus	-	-	-
Producer Surplus	+	+	+
Gross income of Farmers	+	+	+
Required Budgetry Amount (EAGGT)	+	+	+
Value Added of the Community	-	-	-
Internal price stability	+	+	+
External price stability	-	-	-
Income Variation between farmers	+	+	+
Regional specialisation	+	+	+
Imports of Agricultural products from third countries	-	-	-

+ = expansionary effect/increase
- = reduction effect /decrease.

Although table 2 says nothing about the magnitude of effects, it is clear, however, that the contrasting signs alone may give rise to a conflict of interests. The effects are not the same for all member states. There are regional differences and differences related to farm size and type. This can only serve to increase the possibilities for differences in opinion. This leads to involved political discussions at the annual price fixing. Already in the period, 1968-1970, such discussions occured in order to keep the policy within the strictures of the deal. A number of examples can be given of cases which led to the adoption of additional measures. The result being that the system became more complicated.

The first complication to this already extended system arose as a result of the devaluation of the French franc in 1969 and the revaluation of the German mark which followed shortly after. The devaluation should have meant a change in the exchange rate against the Unit of Account, and this should have meant an increase in the price of agricultural products for the french consumer and higher incomes for the french farmers. The french government did not think this advisable. The maintenance of the old rate of exchange against the European Unit of Account was however not possible just like that. The Intervention price in EUA and in francs remained the same, but on exporting to Germany the picture was different. By offering the french wheat to Intervention boards in Germany the old price in EUA and in DM could be obtained, these marks could then be changed at any bank into more francs than before. Exports would thus be worthwhile. Supplies could become dangerously low in France and the German Intervention boards would be flooded with french produce. Order in the market would be upset. To prevent this, a border levy equal to the size of gains from the exchange rate change was instituted between France and the other member states. Member states exporting to France were given a subsidy equal to the border levy. These payments at the border are called Monetary Compensatory amounts. It was intended that these MCA's should only be temporary.

The revaluation of the DM caused similar problems.Adjusting the rates of exchange against the EUA implied less marks per EUA; meaning that German farmers would receive lower incomes. Such a reduction was not seen as desirable by the German government. The same price as before in EUA was paid on goods exported to Germany, and the same number of marks, but this could easily be exchanged for other currencies and exchange rate variation gains be made. In order to prevent difficulties arising in the market, imports were slowed down by introducing a border levy again equal to the exchange rate gains. Exports from Germany received a subsidy of the same magnitude.

Thus, both positive and negetive MCA's were introduced. Since exchange rate variations continued and became infact more frequent these MCA's remained in force, and were readjusted every week in periods of high currency unrest (floating). On the formation of the EMS the EUA was replaced by the ECU, which is a weighted average of the exchange rates of all the currencies of the member states. Every exchange rate change works through to the ECU and this affects the prices of agricultural products.

The level of the MCA's must be continually readjusted. The prices in national currency had a different trend in each of the member states. Uniformity of market prices has thus been lost, see fig. 3.

Another example of the transgression of the limiting conditions occurred around 1970 and was a consequence of the fact that the guaranteed price policy had led to the growth in surpluses, which implied high budgetry expenses, but not the desired level of incomes for farmers. In order to fulfill the clause calling for 'reasonable incomes, reasonable prices and increases in productivity', an attempt was made to bring about a complete modernisation and restructuralisation of agriculture (Mansholt Plan). To achieve this, agricultural employment had to be reduced by about 50%, farm-area by about 7% and some capital be transferred to other production areas. The remaining agricultural resources should be organised into large modern units. Such farms should mean that farmers would obtain reasonable incomes at the existing price levels, without having undesirable effects on supply or the consumer be forced to pay too high prices. International trade would also not be negatively affected. With this in mind, the Mansholt plan was born; however, because of enormous political opposition, no effective large scale structural measures were actually undertaken.
Guidelines on measures for pensioning off and re-educating farmers, and for interest subsidies on some forms of modernisation investment, all to be conducted on a national level, was all that emerged.
It became clear that the hill-farmers could never receive reasonable incomes via the guaranteed price system without over-riding the stated aim regarding prices to consumers and meaning unnecessarily high farm incomes in other areas. But it was not always socially desirable to leave these people without additional governmental support. It was felt that neither the social environment nor the rural beauty (through erosion) of the hilly areas should be allowed to be destroyed. Thus, the so called hill-farm regulation came into being.
Clearly the community responsibility for the financing of the policy has become an increasingly important element in the discussion regarding market regulation. The need has emerged to limit the applicability of price guarantees somewhat, by such diverse measures as premiums on non-delivery of milk, premiums on cattle slaughter, consumer subsidies

Fig. 3 Uniform market prices?

Trend in agricultural prices denominated in national currencies in relation to the EUA, ECU respectively Kuiper (1982).
1. Italy, 2. Ireland, 3. United Kingdom, 4. France, 5. Denmark, 6. Greece, 7. Belgium, 8. Luxembourg, 9. The Netherlands, 10. Germany, EEC = 100.

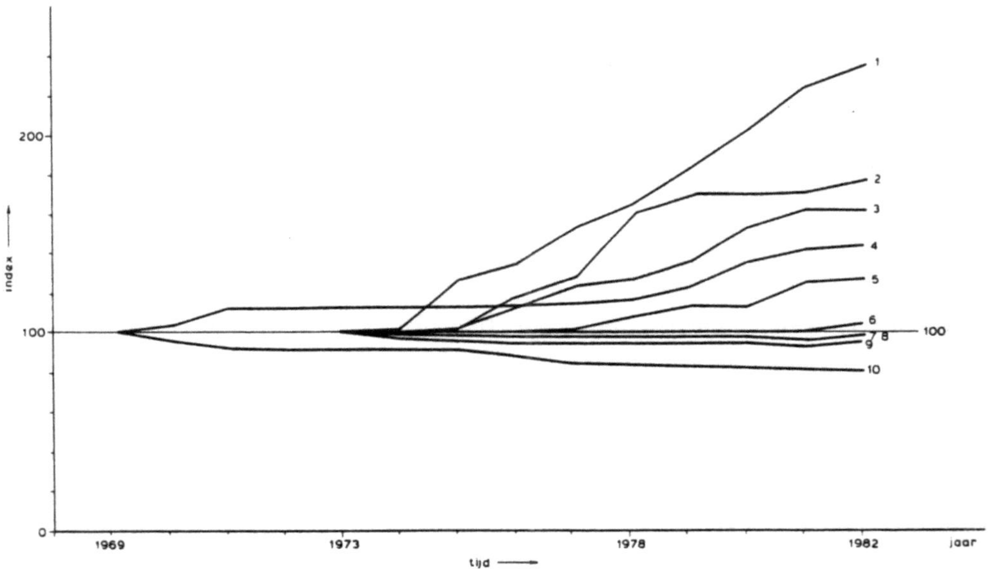

for butter, milk powder and school milk. Additionally, in the case of milk, lower intervention prices apply for quantities, over and above a certain production ceiling. This reduction of the marginal price is called the 'Coresponsibility levy'. Should this prove insufficient, super levies and the suspension of Intervention have been proposed. This implies that the cover of the guarantee would be limited.

The target price is decisive in determining the production in each member state, but not exclusively so: Change in costs of course also has a role to play. So a part of the EEC market is also to be won by the promotion of technical improvement of agriculture and the agricultural marketing system.
Since article 39 of the treaty of Rome seems to place so much importance on the improvement of agricultural productivity one, should perhaps expect that a developed policy should have emerged aiming to promote agricultural technology, or to improve the structure of agriculture. There have been some measures for the improvement of land allocation, and of the markets and marketing channels. But these guidance measures are of limited applicability both technically and financially: In 1979, for example, whilst 9582m ECU were allocated from the European Fund to Agriculture, only 396 m ECU were for guidance measures directed to improve the structure of agriculture. Furthermore, policy regarding the technical development of agriculture is left up to the national authorities.
The system is therefore fundamentally a market and price policy with a guarantee which is in principal unlimited. Since 1977, the financial cost of this policy has accounted for about three-quarters of the total EEC budget. The 10 to 15 mld ECU were financed from the levies on agricultural products, other customs duties and payments from the member states of a small part (max. 1%) of national VAT receipts. So there is a upper limit for the budgetary means of the CAP.
The financing is the subject of political pressure since it is through this channel that the agricultural policy can be modified and also since some states believe that their contributions are too high, whilst others try to use it to increase the real power of the European Parliament. On balance, France, the Netherlands, Ireland and Denmark seem to be net recepients (contributions of 1 to 2 mld. ECU altogether) from the European Fund and the other states (especially Germany) net contributors. Those to benefit being thus the agricultural exporters of the EEC.

4 RESULTS AND PROSPECTS

The 'deal' contained a guarantee for France for the disposal of its grain (and other agricultural products) on the EEC market at a reasonable fixed price. This guarantee was in principal for unlimited quantities. Precaution also had to be taken that agriculture did not stagnate (productivity had to rise), nor should farmers receive unreasonable incomes or consumers have to pay unreasonable prices: and just as trade in agricultural products from third countries should not be excessively interfered with, neither should the supply to European consumers be disrupted.
Was this agreement kept?
Table 3 shows the way in which French production (with a guaranteed market) seems to have developed.

Table 3 French production and disposal 1960-1978

	1960	1967	1978	
Grains	23	32	46	m.ton
	33	36	39	% of EEC
Sugar Beet	19	12	25	m.ton
	33	20	20	% of EEC
Milk	23	27	31	m.ton
	26	28	28	% of EEC

Source: Selected Agrifigures of the EEC 1976 and 1980.

The French share of the EEC market has thus been guaranteed, as has the expansion of this share. In absolute terms, the expansion of the quantity has been very great indeed. It seems that in this period the total EEC market for agricultural products has grown greatly, this has also been the case for the economy as a whole. National incomes have increased greatly in real terms (in total and also per head). It is common knowledge that German industry has expanded. The main aims of the 1950's deal have thus been realised. Has it been possible to achieve this within the bounds set by the limiting conditions? The answer is I suppose yes.
Agriculture has not become stagnant by the price guarantee policy. There has been a high cut back of about 3.9% per year in the numbers of those employed in agriculture. The number of workers per 100 hectares and the

total number of farms has fallen. The structure of agriculture was improved and technical productivity in agriculture has risen greatly, at a pace at least equal to improvements in industry.
Detailed information on farm incomes is not available, but from what is known we may deduce that incomes per head in agriculture have grown as fast as those in the economy as a whole. So absolute incomes are much improved, although the relative position of agricultural incomes has in general been little changed. The statistics in table 4 can be used to give an overall impression. These figures do not suggest that one can talk about unreasonable interference with agricultural incomes.

Table 4 Income per head of the working population of the EEC

	1961	1968	1978
A Agriculture	4000	6700	15500 guilders
B Economy as a whole	10153	19040	39530 guilders
Ratio A'B	39%	35%	39%

Source: Selected Agrifigures 1963, 1970 and 1980

Prices of Agricultural products to the consumer have not risen faster than prices of food and food prices have not risen faster than prices of other products as measured by cost of living indices. One can perhaps conclude from this that the price developments have not been unreasonable as far as the consumer is concerned (see table 5).

Table 5 Annual price increases in percentages 1963-1977

Country	Farm prices	Food prices	All consumer prices
Belgium	4.6	5.8	5.9
Denmark	7.2	8.7	7.5
France	6.0	6.7	6.5
Germany	2.2	3.6	4.0
Italy	-	8.4	8.3
Netherlands	4.1	6.0	6.7
United Kingdom	9.2	9.2	9.1

Source: Meester (1980) p.126

Supply to the internal market is measured in terms of the degree of self-sufficiency, see table 6.

Table 6 The degree of self-sufficiency of the EEC

	1959'61	1976'78
Wheat	78	100
Sugar	96	113
Potatoes	101	98
Vegetables	100	92
Fruit	86	66
Beef	91	97
Pork	98	100
Eggs	95	100
Butter	86	111
Cheese	98	103

Source: Selected Agrifigures 1976 and 1980

These figures show a large production in relation to actual consumption. This security of food consumption excludes possible blockades, boycotts or periods of war. Production remains dependent on the undisturbed import of food energy, fertilizers and such and it is also assumed that transport systems within Europe are not interrupted. In time of war this may not be the case.

International trade has not been reduced following the formation of the customs union, the opposite has occured. Trade between member states increased greatly, but not at the cost of third countries. These were also able to expand deliveries to Europe, although perhaps not as much as would have been the case had no market and price policy been conducted. This created frictions with USA and New Zealand and a number of developing countries. This is to say also that CAP has got an important influence on foreign relations of the EEC.

All in all then the limiting conditions laid down by article 39 of the Treaty of Rome have not been transgressed in achieving the original deal regarding agricultural products (in particular grains). In setting up an EEC agricultural policy the intention was not just to find a solution to agricultural problems in the EEC but to use it as a means of enabling

any form of Economic Integration at all. Should this integration be achieved then an important step had been made on the road to enduring peace and security in Europe, which would also increase welfare. In order to achieve this a special agricultural policy had to be developed which could induce France to take part in the Integration.
Seen as a whole this would improve the social, economic and political situation in Europe, but that doesn't mean that the best possible regulation for agriculture has been made. A deal by its very nature implies that whilst you gain on the one hand, you lose on the other. The general interest may be served by this, but this doesn't imply that the outcome is attractive for every country or political grouping. Furthermore it is not true that the original deal remains equally important for all sides not even for France. Today there is not even a close correlation between the results of CAP and the farming interests of various member countries. The CAP creates burdens as well for the EC as a whole as for the member states. This problem of suboptimality, however, must not be overestimated, because the net welfare change of the CAP was on the average only, about 100 ECU per caput. The social costs of the CAP consisting of the consumers surplus and the producers surplus, are on the average only 30 ECU per caput, or not more than 0.5 per cent of GNP.
The main effect of the CAP is redistribution of income. Gross income of farmers has increased by about 20 per cent at the expense of consumers and taxpayers. This income transfer amounts about 2.5 per cent of GNP. Distribution of income and of taxmoney constitute always political problems. That is also the case for the CAP, especially its budget costs have always been heavily discussed.

The 'Great Grain deal' had no great role to play in the expansion of the EEC to include England, Ireland, Denmark and Greece. For them it is a community attainment, which is not unalterable, if the circumstances or interests require they feel free to bargain. Is is bound to come up for discussion again on the entrance of Spain and Portugal. The question is as to whether a new political accord is possible. Again, just as with France and Germany in their time, it is above all a political matter: The necessity of ensuring democracy on the Iberian Peninsula.

The future seems to hold changes for agriculture. The most immediate modification being the restriction of guaranteed prices to cover only a limited level of production. Already at the yearly price-fixing debate figures for the limitation of production have been considered. Limitation could be introduced in several guises. The discussion about this will have to cover the problems of whether production quotas should apply per farm, per region, per country or for the ECC as a total. Also the question as to how far social payments can be used to improve farm incomes will undoubtably be raised more often than hitherto.

Decision-making within the Common Agricultural Policy takes place in the European Council, on the basis of proposals put forward by the Commision. These proposals are discussed and evaluated in the European Parliament, but not decided upon! The Council is made up of national Ministers of Agriculture in this case. In the decision-making national interests play an important role. The accepted practice of unanimity in deciding upon matters of vital interest such as agricultural policy means that large scale fundamental modification, by which even only one country would lose out, cannot be expected, unless European Integration exhibits dynamism anew and the necessity or possibility of a new deal now with regard to Spain and Portugal emerges.

LITERATURE

ANDREWS, S., Agriculture and the Common Market (Iowa State University Press), 1973.

BOURRINET, J., Le problème agricole dans l'intégration européenne, (Editions Cujas), 1963.

BRITTEN, D.K., National Policies within the CAP Food Policy, 1976, p.405.

BUCHHOLZ, H.E. et.al., Die agrarwirtschaftliche Integration Europas (Nomis Verlag) Baden Baden, 1979.

CAIRNCROSS, A. et.al., Wirtschaftspolitik für Europa, Wege nach vorn, (Piper Verlag, München), 1974.

CHOMBART DE LAUWE, J., L'aventure agricole de la france (Puf)Paris, 1979.

COFFEY, P., editor, Economic policies of the Common Market (Macmillan), London, 1979.

FARNSWORTH, H,C. & K.J. FRIEDEMAN, French and EEC Grain Policies, Stanford Food Research Institute Studies Vol. VII (1), 1967.

FENNELL, R., The common agricultural policy of the European Community, London (Granada), 1979.

HARVEY, D.R., National interests and the CAP, Food Policy, August 1982.

HOOGH, J. DE, De gemeenschappelijke landbouwmarkt, LEI-Jaarverslag 1975. Den Haag, 1976.

KOESTER, U., The redistributional effects of the common agricultural financial system. European Review of Agricultural Economics 4, (1977), 4 p.321.

KUIPER, A.D., Hoe gemeenschappelijk zijn de gemeenschappelijke landbouw-prijzen? Landbouwkundig Tijdschrift 94, (1982), 66.

LABOHM, H.H.J., Europese Dilemma's, ISEI-Pre-advies, Den Haag, 1982.

LIERDE, J. VAN, Europese landbouwproblemen en Europese landbouwpolitiek, (Standaard) Antwerpen, 1967.

LOUWES, S.L. et al., Het EEG landbouwbeleid, (Martinus Nijhof), Den Haag, 1970.

MACKERRON, G. & H.J. RUSH, Agriculture in the EEC, Taking Stock, Food Policy, 1976, p.286.

MALGRAIN, Y., L'intégration agricole de l'europe des six (Edition Cujas), Paris, 1965.

MEESTER, G., Doeleinden, instrumenten en effecten van het landbouwbeleid in de EG (Landbouw-Economisch Instituut), Den Haag, 1980.

NOORT, P.C. VAN DEN, De noodzaak en effectiviteit van het Nederlandse landbouwbeleid en Marshall-Plan tot Mansholt-Plan, Wageningen, 1971. Economic Theory, intuition and the CAP, Food Policy 6 (2), 1981.
OSKAM, A.J., Policy models for the dairy sector of the European Community and the Netherlands, Wageningen, 1981.
PELKMANS, J., Mogelijkheden en voorwaarden voor verdere Europese integratie, ISEI-Pre-advies, Den Haag, 1982.
RODEMER, H., Die EG-Agrarpolitik (Kieler Studien, 164), Tübingen, 1980.
SCHMIDT-VOLKMAR, A., Die Rationalität der Europäischen Agrarpolitik, (Van der Hoeck) Göttingen, 1967.
SELECTED AGRI-FIGURES OF THE EEC, (Min. of Agriculture and Fisheries) The Hague, 1970, 1976, 1980.
SWANN, S., The economics of the Common Market (Penguin), 1970.
SWINBANK, A., The 'objective method': A critique, Eur. Rev. of Agr. Econ., 1979, p.303.
TRACY, M., Agriculture in Western Europe, London, 1964.
VEER, J. DE, The objective method, Eur. Rev. of Agr. Econ. 1979, p.279.

P A R T   T W O

INDUSTRIAL POLICIES AND THE COMMUNITY

by

Alexis Jacquemin

Background

An entire generation of Europeans have lived through the unprecedented period of post-war prosperity. In the years between 1950 and 1972, growth averaged about 5% annually and unemployment stayed below 4%. Living standards surged, and world trade blossomed as never before. People came to consider as a "right" regular wage increases and to increasingly look to governments for a guarantee of the good life with a wide array of social programs (generous old-age pensions, broad medical coverage, education loans, unemployment insurance and so on).

In this context, the creation of the Common Market and the accompanying removal of the diverse obstacles to competition have been welcome.

New attitudes appeared which favoured changes in the structures of economic sectors and businesses, the launching of new industrial initiatives and the acceptance of an automatic and continuous process of adjustment to changing national and international market conditions. The major adjustment problems were those of avoiding "worker alienation" in boring jobs and of improving labour mobility so that peasants, shopkeepers and craft workers would be more willing to move in order to fill positions in the burgeoning sectors of modern, large-scale industry and distribution[1].

In the 1970's however, various "supply-side" shocks[2] suggested that in the 1950's and the 1960's, the Western economies benefited from a great number of conditions which in retrospect seem unique. All industrial countries faced a massive *rise in the real price of raw materials inputs* (both

Coffey, P. (ed.): Main Economic Policy Areas of the EEC
©1983. Martinus Nijhoff Publishers, The Hague / Boston / London
ISBN 90-247-2793-6.

fuel and nonfuel) after 1970, following two decades of falling real input prices. Cheap petroleum was a major catalyst of the postwar boom but it created a pervasive energy dependence throughout the industrial world, which today constitutes a dangerous source of insecurity. Furthermore the two dramatic increases in oil prices, in 1973 and 1979 have had an important deflationary effect because of the partly un-recycled transfer to OPEC. The rising prices of raw material have also had an important impact. Examining the manufacturing sectors of four major industrial countries (U.S., U.K., Germany and Japan), a study concludes that the observed slowdown in manufacturing productivity is largely due to the relative increase in raw material prices - including oil, but not primarily oil, nor even energy. This analysis suggests that the higher raw material prices reduce productivity directly (by reducing the amount of raw materials per unit of labour) as well as indirectly through reduced profits, and therefore capital formation[3].

Accompanying these shocks (and maybe partly explained by them) was a persistent *slowdown in total factor productivity growth* in almost all of the OECD. Another shock has been the rapid *expansion of the newly industrializing countries* (NIC) into traditional export sectors of the Western economies such as steel, shipbuilding, electronic components.

These phenomena were signals for changes and adaptation : higher raw material prices and competition from the NIC's call for sectoral reallocation of resources, as well as overall wage and price adjustments. In the present environment, though, *rigidities* built up during the golden sixties have played a dangerous role. Power has become more concentrated in large corporations, labour unions and lobbying groups. It is the emergence of what J. Lesourne[4] calls a *social oligopoly*, a situation where social groups have become organized to negotiate among themselves or with governments. It is clear that social oligopoly has direct impacts on the structural adjustment of industry, since most structural changes call for transfers of resources from one sector to another and the strategies of the players in the social oligopoly are intended to interfere with this process of reallocation. A well known illustration is the appearance of a "classical" type of unemployment due to the fact that the marginal cost of labour is considered by enterprises to be greater than the marginal value of additional output. Similarly, the income-maintenance mechanisms used by the different social groups during inflation, lead to adjusted expectations contributing to sustain inflation. The *growth of government* and of the public sector deficits is another dimension of these rigidities. It is particularly striking that the relative size of the public sector has grown more rapidly than ever in the post-1973 period. Most government programmes are indeed not sensitive to the kind of market signals which govern private spending, and some programmes are, of course, deliberately contrived to increase as growth slows and unemployment rises.

It is therefore not surprising that over the past decade, heavy tax and wage burdens, along with sluggish growth, have cut deeply into business profits. Confronted by lagging profits and steep interest rates, companies have been forced to reduce their spending for *capital investment*. One consequence is that the growth of investment in industry has slowed down markedly in virtually all industrialized countries since 1973. It is most probable that the rate of growth of the gross stock of business fixed capital has also declined. This fall-off in capital spending is all the more worrisome in the face of the enormity of the industrial restructuring that is necessary.

From that point of view, there are various indications that the performance of Community industry vis à vis two of its principal industrialized trading partners, the U.S.A. and Japan, has not been satisfying[5]. The following aspects can be underlined.

1. Not only are Community exports relatively unspecialised, the *degree of specialisation* in high technology, high skill products seems to be declining and certain Member States' exports are even specialising in product areas where they are - or will be - competing mainly with newly industrial-

ising countries.

2. Analysis of company accounts reveals a *weaker performance in terms of sales margins*, return on assets and remuneration of equity capital by Community companies than by U.S., and to a lesser extent, Japanese companies.

3. European investment in manufacturing has a much lower rate of growth than the Japanese one : in 1980, *investment in manufacturing* as a percentage of GDP was almost twice as high in Japan as in the Community.

In this context, various authors have discussed the dangers of a trend to *de-industrialisation* in Europe[6]. Although there are plenty of arguments concerning the meaning of this concept the main idea is that after the shift from agriculture to industry, there would be a shift from industry to the service-government sector. Such a trend could be regarded as showing a long-run structural feature of advanced industrial countries reaching a certain level of "industrial maturity". It would then be necessary to wonder what the growth potential of these economies will be, given the dynamic role of the manufacturing sector compared with the service sector; what the effects will be on the balance of payments of these nations which could become less able to sell enough of their products abroad to pay for their import requirements; what the consequences will be for safeguarding a socially acceptable level of employment.

Today, the reactions of the various economic agents are still uncertain.

At the level of *national governments*, one notes an increasing degree of interference in national productive activity and in international trade which have led to a renaissance of diverse forms of protectionism.

At the level of *national entreprises*, oligopolistic structures become evident through the high level of industrial concentration[7]. These structures gradually become embedded in national and international markets just as the more traditional types of international cartels tend to lose their efficiency. Also, in order to reduce the uncertainty of the market, there is an increase in collusion between these large businesses and the public authorities. This quest for short-term security is evident from the multitude of planning agreements between state and private enterprises, and assistance for sectors and companies in difficulties which cannot be expected to cope with national Community and international competition. Such an evolution tends to favour political processes of reallocation of resources at the expense of market mechanisms.

At the level of *multinational enterprises*, there is the danger of a new generation of European oligopolistic multinationals which are neither responsive to national governments nor to the EEC institutions. In the face of the crisis, these multinationals show themselves to be capable of reducing the instability of their activities - but at the price of destabilising their local environment by transferring risks to the local markets where they are operating[8].

Thus there is a shifting balance between contradictory tendencies - especially between deliberate control of European economies on the one hand, and the maintenance of competition as the principle motor of economic activity on the other.

In effect, the two movements may be observed. On the one hand, there is in many circles a desire to maintain the decentralized forces of a competitive economic system which assure a constant adaptation to changes in needs, techniques and general economic conditions and which assure the maintenance of risk-taking and industrial dynamism. On the other hand, there is a growing desire - equally among national governments, private businesses and workers - to avoid the ups-and-downs of economic activity and to reduce uncertainty through direct collaboration between the private and public sectors.

It would seem to be unrealistic to expect a clear choice to be made between these contradictory tendencies during the coming years. A realistic attitude towards European industry should rater move in the following ways. One would be to seek means of limiting the number of sectors in which competition is obstructed; equally, the duration of such obstruction should be reduced. The other way would be to coordinate, at the level of the Community - for those sectors where for economic or social reasons such obstruction is inevitable - national measures of intervention and planning agreements.

It is with the preceding considerations in mind that we shall examine successively the main types of industrial policy and their limits (Section 1), the evolution which may be observed in European industrial policy (Section 2) and, finally some perspectives for the future (Section 3).

1. Market and Directive Industrial Policies

The main characteristics of an industrial policy is that it has to specify and solve the problems of structural change in the economy. Its task is to create optimum conditions for the necessary structural transformations to be carried out. The need for transformation arises from changes occuring in the process of industrial development : technological changes, shifts in demand, maturing and declining industries, and so on. The required adaptations take time, so that industrial policy is essentially long-term. Beyond this background, there are divergent views whether they concern aims or the means used.

Concerning aims, some would see them as the instruments intended to allow competition to function completely efficiently. According to L. Stoleru, industrial policy may be defined as being "a policy of coordinating the actions of the public authorities in the direction of maximising the virtues of a competitive economy"[9]. Similarly, Toulemon and Flory assume that with regard to industrial policy, the role of the public authorities is to establish "the framework within which the activities of producers and the choice of consumers are facilitated"[10].

Others, on the contrary, believe that industrial policy should have a more voluntarist character. It would thus be seen as being a number of means used by the public authorities to channel industrial activity in the framework of a general economic programme towards a number of pre-established objectives[11].

1.1. Competition-orientated Industrial Policy

1.1.1. If we accept the concept whereby industrial policy is intended to free the potentialities of the decentralised economy, its role can be seen as creating an environment that facilitates the use of the best of the forces of competition. Equally, a related automatic and continuous process of industrial adjustment will be facilitated.

Concerning industrial concentration, this competition policy favour industrial regroupings or cooperation between small and average-sized enterprises, in such a way that they grow to the optimum size for being effective partners in the market.

Regarding barriers to entry into a sector, this policy removes artificial obstacles such as differences of technical norms, discriminating fiscal charges, public markets divided into branches, and conditions of unequal financing. Also, concerning the differentiation of products, efforts should be made to improve information and to protect the consumer.

In general, it is important to reinforce the active industrialist who alone can give life to a competitive enterprise if the economic and social climate allows it. Such a system presupposes an infrastructure of quality, a professionally adapted manual labour force, accessibility of capital and credit, and a fiscal system which is not opposed to economic rationality.

This tendency, which is opposed to dirigism, does not on the contrary exclude some state action and the use of strategy on the part of the enterprises. It does not refuse the requirements of the competitive system, even if it is admitted that they must sometimes be moderated. Thus, regarding French industrial policy, H. de L'Estoile[12] speaks of a "free muscled exchange". But with certain reservations, industrial policy that we shall call a "market" one rests soundly on the constraints of the competitive process. Private enterprises, by their investment and production decisions, remain the main protagonists in industrial evolution. In turn, public authorities facilitate efficient decisions and ensure an environment propitious to healthy functionning of the decentralised system.

1.1.2. The limits of this policy are numerous and it is enough to distinguish between two types, one at the domestic level, the other at the foreign level.

At the domestic level, the market economy is beset with important failures that explain the desire for a more interventionist industrial policy. Let us enumerate the principal failures :

The regional imbalance and differences in development are less and less accepted, but could be accentuated by the free circulation of people, assets and capital. As shown by J. Meade[13], if different citizens start with different endowments of factors of production, then the forces of competition can lead to greater inequalities in the absence of any governmental intervention to make the gainers compensate the losers.

The social costs, combined with the mobility of resources and especially of employment, are often considered to be intolerable to such a degree that only the mediation of the State is capable of safeguarding a minimum of organised institutionalised mobility.

The responsibility for the degradation of the environment is not spontaneously accepted by industry, but represents an increasing cost for society.

Linked with the preceding phenomenon, the assets and services of the community that concern urban development, green spaces, or security, are not taken into account by the market economy.

The dynamics of the system presuppose a permanent renewal of industrial initiatives, which implies an elastic supply of business talent, when in effect at the moment one has the impression that business initiative is on the decline. Thus, firms die and are not replaced, and this situation could threaten the existence of competitive self-regulation. One of the essential causes of this temporary failure is the particularly high risks of entering a market as a result of the multiple uncertainties that affect the capital and money markets, and those for raw materials and labour.

The new technological industries are characterised by a high degree of research; increasing returns of scale and other considerations encourage a regrouping and concentration of means that threaten the competitive system.

All these aspects are reasons why the price system may fail to emit correct signals on economic scarcity and require industrial adaptation, such failures being magnified in an inflationary context[14]. Indeed theory and evidence show that inflation increases the variability of *relative* prices. The price information becomes less valuable and uncertainty is increased. Then, resource allocation processes, to be efficiently carried out, must be based upon non-price signals, alternative market mechanisms, or non-market institutions replacing, at a cost, the market.

Even if correct signals are emitted, economic agents could not react to them hoping to gain security in the short run. This sluggishness of reaction could be worsened by a decrease of the supply elasticity of entrepreneurial talent and of its transferability, as previously mentioned.

At the foreign level, the limits of the international division of labour present a threat. This division is confronted with the advantages of a minimum level of national autonomy below which national security would be threatened. The oil crisis, the tendency of the countries producing raw materials to reduce their supply and to transform the materials at home, the hazy character of the industrial list of initial and anticipated comparative advantages, the necessary structural adjustments and the transformation of entire sectors - all these make less realistic, at least at the socio-political level, a system that would leave to market forces the solution of such problems.

In the light of multiple criteria and in a dynamic perspective, the acceptance of the model of free exchange and of the Pareto-optimality character of its implications is much less evident. As long as there exists no mechanism to ensure that world cooperation - leading to a maximisation of the common surplus - is possible and would be stable, in as far as this solution also gives more to certain partners and is not reinforced by systems of international redistribution of profits (side-payments) effecting transfer from the more favoured to the less favoured, it is understandable that States hesitate to accept a specialisation leading to the maximum degree of international openness. They could be tempted to adopt individual policies of the "maximin" type - at the risk of these latter leading to results which could be fatal for the collective equilibrium[15].

1.2. Directive Industrial Policy

1.2.1. It is clear that there exists a place nowadays for an industrial policy of intervention which does not restrict itself to giving to the market economy its full effectiveness, but which sets a certain number of priority objectives for the industrial activity in the private and public sectors.

The means used to achieve this are many and can be coercive in nature or able to stimulate changes. In the first case, preference is given to systems of quotas, to rationing, or to imposed prices. In the second case, one attempts to make profitable the adoption by the economic agents concerned of the policies desired by the public authorities. Thus one uses subsidies, allowances, or relief from taxation. In particular, if the government is more neutral toward risk than the private investor, it subsidises the projects in order to further the level of investment. Such neutrality could be justified as long as the total cost of risk-bearing of an independent project is made negligible by the spreading of the risk over the entire population of taxpayers. It is here also that the various forms of contracts for restructuring and encouraging business management come in, ensuring that, in exchange for the subsidies transferred by the public authorities, the enterprises agree to contribute to the achievement of the sectoral, technological and regional objectives of the Plan. For example, the enterprise has to realise investments enabling it to increase its production capacity or to maintain the level of employment; and, in exchange, it benefits from budgetary credits; or an organ of the State (Société Nationale d'Investissement in Belgium, National Enterprise Board in Great Britain, Institut de Développement Industriel in France, GEPI, IRI and ENI in Italy,...) will take a direct participation in the firm.

This brings us to a second level : the State, whether in collaboration with the private sector or alone, takes on productive activities, through the medium of its public enterprises or mixed enterprises; it can thus influence industrial structures direclty. Apart from the sectors where the competition of the private sector is no longer applicable because the increase in production leads to increasing returns and subsequently to the formation of a monopoly, its field of action can extend to the production of strategic goods and services whose importance for the national economy is such that it cannot remain in the hands of the private sector (for example, credits and energy). Besides, the sectors normally reserved for private enterprise can equally become a potential field for State participation to assure a better sectoral division of investment. In particular, this concerns investments of which the economic risk is too big for the private sector alone, or, even more, investments that have great technical importance for the whole economy (pace-making sectors).

With this in view, most West European governments and especially France have introduced *new public enterprises* since the late 1960's which are devoted to the management of industry. In general, these second-generation public enterprises contrast with earlier nationalisations in that governments consciously sought participation in viable and competitive rather than in failing concerns[16].

1.2.2. But the voluntarist industrial policy presents, in its turn, certain limits which can be summed up by the following dilemma : should one submit to the demands of efficiency generally linked with international conditions of competition and risk losing the means of control linked with the responsibility of public interest; or should one fix public objectives with the danger of misguided actions or the creation of big "white elephants"?

More precisely, the choices for industrial redevelopment are not selfevident and - apart from some general themes such as the move towards products of great value-added, depending on an advanced technology and incorporating little energy - exact criteria are lacking.

As Malinvaud stated during the Paris colloquium on industrial redevelopment, "You cannot expect, in any particular case, that economic studies will give incontestable indications as to which branches should be developed"[17] .

Difficulties can also arise at the level of large-scale projects. Thus, at all times, the European public authorities have encouraged large enterprises as a means of responding to the challenge of America or even of Japan. It is only recently that scepticism has appeared on the subject of the *link between the size of firms and the quality of their performance*.

Indeed, as far as the effects of large European size is concerned, no evidence of increasing profit, faster growth, or more intensive research activities, can be found to support the "size mystique" that has prevailed in Europe[18] .

Equally, public authorities are too often confined to the role of giving social assistance to enterprises in difficulty An obvious case is the conflict that arose in 1967 in Belgium between the State on the one side and the National Association of Industrial Credit (SNCI) on the other. This organisation wished, according to its initial responsibility, to give help to new industrial initiatives; instead of which it was forced to support condemned enterprises. Finally the government forced on the SNCI the conclusion of a convention (9 May 1968) allowing the granting of credits to enterprises in difficulty.

Finally, public industrial initiative can become a kind of "corporatist" system, with nomination of employees for political reasons, lacking a sense of responsibility and initiative, and not subject to the discipline of competition and of profitability, (public enterprises which are badly managed do not usually disappear by way of the Bankruptcy Courts).

1.3. Mixed Industrial Policies in Mixed National Economies

In our mixed economies, the contrast between market and directive industrial policies is theoretical. In fact, there is a *continuum* in the degree of interventionism. In each European country, some industrial sectors are affected by public microeconomic measures to prevent or to promote a structural change, while simultaneously other sectors are freely submitted to the market system. Similarly, when comparing two countries such as Germany and France, the two corresponding industrial policies are officially quite different, the first one being of the market type and the second one of the interventionist type. In fact they are very similar in everyday practice, particularly if the differences between the national industrial structures are taken into account.

Contrasting with these mixed national industrial policies, one can say that, until now, the European industrial policy has been a pure market policy. It has tried to play the role of a useful complement vis à vis the antitrust policy in favouring the realisation of an integrated market between member states. In most cases, the action of the Commission has been counter-interventionist, that is to say, it has limited excessive governmental intervention in the functioning of the Common Market. Diverse phenomena, catalysed by the crisis and mentioned in the introduction, have brought this perspective into question and have led to the renewal of the call for a more voluntarist industrial policy, as was expressed in the CECA and Euratom Treaties, and as was conceived by certain promoters of European medium-term programming. Equally, the virtues of the competitive system, both inside the Community and in its relations with third parties, have been questioned, and, as a result, the industrial and competitive European policies, clashed more and more frequently, both among themselves, and with the corresponding national policies. The basic questions have then become : in terms of Community cohesion, are the political benefits of developing a "mixed" European industrial policy including limited measures of protection on a Community-wide basis, worth the economic cost to efficient producers inside and outside the Community ? Is it the view that will be adopted by the European Authorities ?

2. In Search of a European Industrial Policy

The Commission of the EEC stated in its ninth general report : "as regards industrial policy we must state that the list of decisions taken at Community level during the year 1975 is still as small as before, in spite of the development of an economic situation which would seem logically to call for the reinforcement of European cooperation".

In this section, we shall briefly describe the origins of the European Industrial Policy and the efforts made to shift from a "European Industrial Market Policy" to a "European Industrial Policy of Intervention".

2.1. While the Treaty of Rome explicitly prescribes the situation relative to common policies in the case of agriculture, competition, employment, commerce, transport, and fiscal harmonisation, there is no reference to industrial policy. However, the *two sectoral treaties of CECA and Euratom indicate* without expressly stating it *the desire to create an industrial policy*. In entrusting to the High Authority powers of supranational management, the Member States have permitted creation of a common strategy in the basic fields which, during the 1950's, meant coal and steel.

Thus, the coal crisis which arose in 1958 was solved by a systematic conversion plan which avoided the principal social tensions that would no doubt have been produced if matters had been left to market forces. Policy for the steel industry had the objective of reducing the economic imbalance between supply and demand, encouraging the reconstruction and modernisation of enterprises, as well as promoting agreements for self-limitation between European, American and Japanses producers.

But some observers could also argue that such cooperation has reduced pressures for rationalisation and specialisation of these activities, making the present crisis worse.

The Treaty instituting the European Atomic Energy Community was above all intended to develop research and encourage industrial initiative in the nuclear field. According to Article 4, "the Commission has the responsibility of promoting and facilitating nuclear research in the Member States and of complementing them by research and training programmes undertaken by the Community". This second Industrial Treaty has not, however, had the same success as the previous one. It was concerned with the promotion of a common programme, either by direct action such as research undertaken in the "Joint Research Centre" (of which the institutions are in Ispra, Mol, Karlsruhe and Petten), or by indirect action in the form of contracts specially aimed at promoting coordination between research centres and national programmes. In fact, these efforts have not really succeeded. On the one hand, the Member States have, for the greater part, preferred to pursue a national policy and to maintain market divisions, resulting in the multiplication of non-coordinated and even competitive programmes. On the other hand, the common programme itself has not given satisfactory results : most of the research has remained at a pre-industrial stage and the main needs of industry have had to be supplied by American technology, without even attaining a comparable level of efficiency. Besides, until the creation of EURODIF, the Community was depending upon foreign sources for its supply of enriched uranium. The Commission in its report of 1968 was forced to conclude : "The Treaty which created the European Community of Atomic Energy aimed at creating conditions favourable to the development of a powerful nuclear industry. After ten years, we must admit that it has only partially attained this objective".

Since the crisis, the Commission is trying to develop an *energy strategy for the Community*. Nuclear research under the Euratom Treaty has been extended to non-nuclear sectors. The Joint Research Centre and the Directorate General for Science

Research and Development, have been brought under a single Directorate General, so that, in the future, a more integrated approach has a better chance to emerge[19] .

In the more general framework of the EEC, the first manifestations of an industrial policy go back to 1964, when the idea of "*a medium-term economic programme*" was introduced. Since the publication of a second programme, prepared in 1965, and covering the period 1968-70, the Commission has insisted on the necessity of public intervention to improve the industrial structures of the Community and has set up a *Directorate for Industrial Policy* which is responsible for the preparation of orientations for the common industrial policy and the coordination of the intervention of the Member States. Besides this, sectoral cooperation with the industrialists, trade unions, and national experts are occasionally organised in various sectors, such as aeronautics, shipbuilding, data-processing, paper, and textiles.

About 1970 the necessity of defining a general industrial policy was clearly and publicly asserted : such is the aim of the Memorandum of the Commission to the Council, entitled *The Industrial Policy of the Community*, EEC Commission, Brussels, 1970. As the authors stated :

> Twelve years after its foundation, whilst the period of transition that led to the liberalisation of the common market of goods has just been completed, the Community approaches a new phase of its construction. The preparation of a common policy for industrial development favouring the constitution of what one could call a European industrial framework becomes indispensable to assure at the same time the irreversible bases for the economic, and soon the political, unity of Western Europe, the pursuance of economic expansion, and a reasonable degree of technological autonomy as regards its main external partners (p.7).

But straight away the authors came up against the actual definition of this policy. They chose a particularly non-interventionist approach : "to allow industry to derive the maximum advantages from the existence and size of the 'Common

Market' (p.9). The ways they hoped to establish this industrial policy included the following :

The achievement of a unified market by the elimination of technical obstacles and the opening-up of the public sectors and the abolition of fiscal frontiers.

The unification of the judicial, fiscal and financial laws.

The restructuring of enterprises through the elimination of the obstacles to the formation of trans-national European enterprises, using to this end public credits for industrial development in the sectors of advanced technology.

The organisation of changes and adaptation by facilitating changing jobs, industrial exploitation of innovation, improvement in the management of enterprises, and in the recruitment of their managers and directors.

The extension of Community solidarity in economic relations with third parties, in particular, by way of the common commercial policy.

In spite of its qualities, the Memorandum gives an impression of dissatisfaction. There is a clear contrast between the wealth of information that it sheds on the situation of the Community's industry and the lack of clarity about the policies proposed. The absence of a precise political engagement did not change the fact that one had to wait until the Declaration of Paris in October 1972 for the governments to express their support for this loose industrial policy.

Apart from the desire to coordinate policies at the Community level and to have a precise timetable and finance settled before 1 January 1974, this declaration was once again expressed in rather general terms. One may be surprised that it has taken so long to arrive at this declaration of principle. Diverse factors delayed the Community's progress in this field. These may be defined as follows :

(a) The quarrel concerning the enlargement of the Community blocked all new developments not originally foreseen, in the meantime, and the negotiations of adherence received priority.

(b) Certain initiatives, especially French ones, have taken inter-governmental scientific and technical cooperation agreements outside the Community sphere (for example, Concorde and the Airbus).

(c) The traditional conflict between the States more attached to liberalism, such as Germany, and those which practise a more interventionist policy, such as France or Italy, has been complicated by a conflict in the attitude towards the United States. In this respect, France is in fact more anxious to affirm the European autonomy vis à vis the United States than are Germany, Italy or the Benelux.

(d) The refusal to make a broad approach and the insistence on the principle of the '*juste retour*' restrict progress.

(e) Finally, a common industrial policy concerning pace-making industries, such as aeronautics, computers or electronics, can only be realised in so far as the Europen Community takes on the political dimension that it still lacks at the present time.

Despite all these considerations, on the basis of the Declaration of Paris, the Commission produced, as from May 1973, the "programme for industrial and technological policy", also called the Spinelli Report. A list of decisions of the Council and of Member States was proposed, the adoption of which the Commission deemed necessary, with a timetable lasting until 1977.

If all the propositions are not yet realised, numerous aspects have been touched upon :

(1) Regarding the elimination of technical obstacles to trade various proposals or directives aim at the harmonisation of national regulations. This harmonisation is not only designed to remove obstacles to trade inside the Community; it should also allow the achievement of qualitative objectives important in the fields of public health and for the protection of the environment. The chemical and pharmaceutical sectors are already the object of diverse measures to assure the opening-up of the market.

(2) The opening-up of national markets for purchasing by public

and semi-public sectors in the Community implies that any "preference" or "reservation" for national production, or any exclusion of deliveries of imported products from other Member States, should be permanently forbidden. One of the propositions of the directives aims, in particular, at the coordination of procedures concerning public tenders. This contains rules governing publicity, going as far as the publication of notification of contracts for tenders in the Official Journal of the Community. The directive concerning public works contracts has already imposed this obligation (26 July 1971).

(3) The encouragement of trans-national European enterprises is desirable and can reinforce competition. "Concentration in the national sphere leads to competition between firms that are supported in diverse ways by their governments and that do not often come to reach the threshold of profitability. The trans-national groupings offer, on the contrary, the possibility of combining effective competition and economies of scale". It is in this perspective that the directives concerning the harmonisation of company law should be seen (in particular that of the limited liability company, the SPRL, the cooperative society, the private company groups of companies, and that concerning consolidated balances), and also the directives aiming to create new juridical forms, such as the European company, the European group for cooperation, and the common enterprise, hitherto reserved exclusively for nuclear field. At the initiative of Mr Vredeling, a new directive is likewise awaited concerning the participation of workers in their enterprises (see OJL, n°C 297/3, 15 November 1980). The same applies to the directives relating to industrial property, fiscal law, and capital markets.

(4) Regarding small and medium-sized enterprises, there exist "Community development contracts designed to support innovations developed through trans-national cooperation, as well as an "Office for Mergers between Enterprises". This office furnishes enterprises with information and advice,

informs the Community about the obstacles of a general nature that the enterprises meet in their attempts to cooperate or to merge together, and seeks partners for the enterprises of different nationalities wishing to engage in cooperation with a view to improving their competitiveness and facilitating their adaptation to the enlarged market. It can also cover cooperation agreements as well as financial integration (common branch offices, participation, merger or absorption).

(5) Concerning the sectors confronted with special problems, the Commission proposes to by-pass the distinction dividing sectors of advanced technology and sectors in the process of change or in trouble. The most serious actual problem concerns a group of sectors, namely those of the heavy investment equipment. It aims at allowing the Community to gauge, in time, the risks it runs in the field of long-term supplies of raw materials, energy and key products. The Commission has decided to undertake a systematic study of primary resources that will be necessary to the Community in the future.

(6) Finally, the necessity of coherence of industrial policy with the other objectives of the Community, in the social, regional and commercial fields is stressed, without making any concrete propositions, as such, with the exception of the work of the Social Fund and of the European Regional Fund. Those play only a marginal role, however.

In his programme speech of 8 February 1977, the President of the Commission particularly insisted on the key problem of the different stages of evolution of the economies and on the necessity of more varied and flexible means than those of the present Funds in order to reduce these divergences[20].

2.2. On examination of the principal aspects of the European industrial policy, it seems clear that, despite the perspective which has guided those responsible, it concerns essentially what we have called a "competition-orientated" industrial policy. By contrast with the experiences of the CECA, and of Euratom, the means used consist of those designed to assure an integrated market.

On the contrary, Mr Marjolin aims, as a start, to complete the mechanisms of the market by means of a European medium term economic programme susceptible of controlling and influencing industrial development. But such an orientation presupposes a solid consensus of European policy, a consensus relying on the rationalisation and the reconversion of sectors in decline, as well as on the common promotion of pace-making sectors.

In reality, it has not been possible to coordinate aid given by States to *sectors in trouble*. Within the context of the crisis, the national public authorities have not waited for the recommendations of Brussels to coordinate their aid, running the risk of simply preserving an obsolete industrial structure or transferring difficulties from one Member State to another. It is this which the successive reports of the Commission about the policy of competition make evident. In the 6th Report[21] one can read a long description of various aid given by States to their enterprises and the difficulty the Commission has in controlling them against a background of economic recession. The question is the more delicate since the so-called "opaque" aids (as compared with "transparent" ones) tend to multiply. These opaque aids that can not be expressed as a percentage of investment (fiscal aids, help for creation of new employment, and for the better functioning of enterprises) represent nearly 50 per cent of the budget devoted to regional policy by the whole of the Member States.

Besides, as we have seen, European initiatives in the *sectors of advanced technology* have been swept away by national actions, unilateral or bilateral; for example, in the electronics industry (with the disappearance of UNIDATA), or in aeronautics as characterised by the achievements of certain countries. The result is the multiplication of non-coordinated, even competitive, programmes. However, even here, the necessity of a common industrial policy is self-evident in so far as these fundamental sectors imply enormous expenses for research and development before becoming profitable, because they must realise economies of scale which only the integrated market permits them to obtain.

In the General Report of the Commission[22] for the year 1976 may be seen the desire for a move from a competitive-orientated industrial policy to more interventionist initiatives. The Commission affirms there that in the actual economic circumstances the action of the Community regarding industrial development could not limit itself to a pure and simple application of the rules of the Treaty of the EEC. It had also to begin to orientate, coordinate and eventually to complete the measures that Member States judged indispensable at national level (p.210).

The two principal lines followed are :

(1) to try to arrive at a common strategy in the pace-making sectors, for which the intervention of States is often crucial;

(2) to coordinate the policies of the Member States in the sectors in difficulties, to prevent them interfering or cancelling reciprocally[23] .

A supplementary stage was reached in the final text of the proposed *Fourth Medium-Term Economic Programme*[24] . One can read there that enterprises should have at their disposal more abundant information concerning current developments. This improved "transparency" of structural changes will encourage a more searching attitude among the managers of enterprises. For that purpose it would be suitable to bring together and to study at Community level the forecasts available at national level concerning the sectoral evolution (p.62). And at Point 9 of the project, it is added that "In order to improve the transparency in certain capital-intensive industrial sectors where there exist risks of overcapacity, the Commission at regular intervals requires *a notification concerning investment projects*" (p.7). Had this proposition of a preliminary notification of investment projects been accepted, it would have been an important step in the direction of concerted industrial policy. But at the level of the Council of Ministers, it ran into strong opposition, emanating mainly from Germany. The case was the more difficult to defend as the steel industry was then in the middle of a crisis. In the decision of the Council of 14 March 1974, laying down the fourth programme, the paragraph in question has been replaced by the following vague text (point 8) : "The Commission will encourage the establishment, at national level, of sectoral analyses that will be examined together by the Member States at Community level. On this occasion, it will be assessed to what degree these analyses may lead to Community decisions[25] .

Today, the Director of the Directorate for Industrial Policy[26] must find a compromise between a "Directive Industrial Policy" and a "Competition-orientated Industrial Policy". Instead of making grandiose declarations of intent, the Commission has tried to prove its political capacity to elaborate European operational plans for the reconversion and expansion of specified sectors : the steel industry, the textile industry (where it has to go well beyond the renewal of the Multifibre Arrangement), aeronautics, the shipping industry and computers. In all cases, "action-programmes" have been worked out.

Various actions have also recently been taken by the Council, in favour of pace-making sectors as well as sectors in difficulties. For example, in the field of *microelectronic technology*, it has adopted a Regulation (OJL 376, 30 December 1981) to provide Community support for projects intended to supply the European industry with highly specialized industrial equipment for the design and manufacture for sub-micronscale integrated circuits, essential building blocks in this sector. It has also adopted the proposal for a fifth Directive on aid to *shipbuilding* to reorganize the sector and increase its efficiency. Subject to certain conditions it allows crisis aid and aid to deal with the social and regional consequences of restructuring (OJL 137, 23 May 1981). In view of the increasing seriousness of the crisis in the *steel industry*, the Council considered that the previous aids Decisions of the

Commission was no longer an adequate instrument and asked the Commission to replace it with a new Decision reflecting the principles of the Resolution that it has adopted in March 1981. This Resolution defined the policy objective as "the restoration in the medium-term of normal market conditions in which undertaking are profitable" and laid down a number of criteria to restrict obtainment of aids (progressive reduction and limited period, notification in advance, full transparency, existence of complete specific plans, no increase of capacity for products for which there was not a growing market). The new Decision was adopted by the Commission in August 1981 (OJL 228, 13 August 1981). However, the desired results are far from being obtained.

It is clear that the future of European steel industry should lie with high added value products, not basic commodity products. It is then necessary to get rid of excess steel making capacities. But the price stability given by the EEC arrangements has precisely created conditions reducing the pressure for restructuring. Furthermore reducing the steelmakers' losses through higher prices has imposed an artificial costs burden on European steel users and manufacturing industry in general. In fact, the steel industry is an illustration of the main difficulties encountered by European industrial policies :

- few of the national aids have corresponded to the letter or the spirit of the Decision (especially as regards the relationship between aid and capacity);
- one does not get the impression of a real desire for common policy but rather for a cartel arrangement implying all the problems of instability and enforcement, since the temptation to cheat is strong (because the returns from cheating are substantial) and the degree of control is weak;
- even in this industry, national production conditions are not homogeneous, the range of products is different from one country to another, and the level of intervention must be more and more disaggregated.

This last difficulty is a very general one and is even more

important in other industries. It is indeed well known that an ever-increasing part of trade between European countries as well as with other countries corresponds with products that belong to the same branches of the industry but which differentiate themselves by their special qualities.

It is then dangerous to expect of the European authorities (as well as of national authorities) systematic orientation of specialisation at this *intra-industrial level*. In effect, if in some sectors the products are standardised, production is concentrated, the statistical information is strongly developed and the habits of dialogue and cooperation (even collusion) firmly rooted, it is not the same for numerous other industries. Besides, the source of difficulties varies from one case to another, ranging from the question of commercial policy to that of financial management.

Finally, microeconomic statistics are, in general, terribly bare and unstandardised. Thus, to expect that European Industrial Policy should stimulate, orientate and control the industrial redevelopment at this level is hazardous. Such a policy, that would in effect tend to duplicate the competitive decentralized process by a badly-informed, badly-equipped "visible hand" working expensively could result in an unmanageable situation.

As illustrated by the case of the steel industry, *it will not be easy for the European Authorities to find their ways between general plans for reconversion and development, and microeconomic industrial policies bringing them into the nitty-gritty of deciding which firm, indeed, which product of the firm, is eligible for access to investment funds, and how those funds should be spent.*

3. General Perspectives

The fifth medium-term economic policy programme which covers the period 1981-1985 is built around two objectives, namely the control of inflation and structural adjustment, these being prerequisites for the lasting creation of new jobs. This programme suggests that the corresponding strategy must be based on the Community's role in implementing specific policies, boosting investment, completing the single market, and pursuing an active employment policy. A recent communication from the Commission to the Council indicates what could be the content of such a strategy with respect to the European industry[27].

The basic idea is that the process of an ever-increasing integration has gradually been slowed down by fragmentation of the internal market due to growing public intervention in the national economies. This trend has discouraged the creation of European companies and groupings, and has weakened our industry's ability to meet the challenges posed by the present crisis. European industry is undeniably handicapped on the international markets by the fact that measures to assist firms are taken in a national framework without any concerted action at Community level. "The Community as such has virtually no instrument at present for promoting either exports or external investments" (p.14). Furthermore, the firm organized on a European scale is often treated with suspicion by governments reluctant to afford it the benefit of their various industrial policy instruments : financing, R and D aid, public contracts, norms and standards, etc. "Thus, for a company to organize itself on a European scale, which ought to be considerable asset in the common market, in fact turns out to be a handicap" (p.16). It is then proposed to add an element of "Community preference" in all the cases where industrial development involves the participation of the public authorities. Various types of measures are then proposed :

- to set *technical norms and standards* for the whole of the Community at once, priority in their establishemnt being able to give European industry an advantage over its competitors;
- to set preferences with regard to public procurement, by creating a European public agency for coordination and execution of a supply policy : one strategic area for such an approach is *telecommunications*, particularly space communication and integrated numerical networks;

- to use the Community own policies (competition, environment, R and D, financial instruments, trade policy) to *give preferences to the development of European companies* : the position adopted by the Commission on the motor vehicle industry is an example of this attitude (see COM(81)317);
- to set up *data banks and industrial performance charts*, giving European producers an integrated frame of reference : in this view the "Euronet system"[28] could provide relevant information to governments and companies on Community market and industrial structural trends.

It would be unfair to argue that these proposals mean a move towards a deliberate protectionism at Community level. Rather it suggests that officials of the European Community, valuing the political solidarity of the EEC, realize that today selective, supranationally supervised, debated and negociated agreements could be a second best policy when compared with a retreat to generalised national protectionism which could cause the desintegration both of the European Community and the GATT system. As underlined by L. Franko (art. cit.), economic theory teaches that the "best" industrial policy would involve the dismantling of the vast majority of the measures currently going on in the name of industrial policy and the strict enforcement of anti-trust rules. But under conditions of discontinuous jumps and shocks considered by the actors involved as exogenous, with increasing structural unemployment, sluggish and costly economic, social and political adjustment, there is a need for constructive European industrial policies helping the Community to reinforce its identity and to move solidarily toward a situation where markets can again work.

Several authors have recently argued that it is necessary to go one step further and to combine industrial and trade policies in order to elaborate a deliberate if moderate external protectionism at Community level, while maintaining competition within the Community[29] . Among the arguments, it is stated that labour in Europe and the U.S. is priced at an artificially high level and that all NICs pursue policies which concentrate development on a limited number of sectors which are subsidised at every level : infra-structure, capital and the export products themselves, plus protection of the home market; that the most vigorous and successful example of industrial policy, that of Japan, is certainly heavily protectionist; that the Community as a whole must conceive itself to be in what amounts to a developmental phase of industrial restructuring. According to this view, anti-dumping duties, selective quotas, crisis cartels, must be included among the tools of industrial policy; higher concentration and mergers must be promoted at the EEC level.

Until now the European Authorities have firmly rejected such a view. A recent example is given in the *Eleventh Report on Competition Policy* (April 1982) which states that *structural crisis cartels* which provide for participation by at least a majority of the undertakings in the sector concerned, compliance with a strict code of internal discipline covering all the economic activities of its members and protection against competition by outsiders, are incompatible with the conditions for exemption provided for in Article 85(3). Similarly, the Commission has submitted to the European Parliament a new proposal for a Regulation on the *merger control*. More generally, the Commission is constantly insisting on the fact that it is an absurd contradiction to predicate Europe's economic expansion on a growth in world trade and at the same time to hold it down on its own market. It is well known that until now trade in industrial goods between industrial and developing countries, including the NIC, have been most beneficial for Europe, in terms of trade balance, employment and price stability. According to prospects for 1978-1990, the export surplus of the industrial countries would even rise[30] indicating our interest in a liberal trade environment. From this point of view, the role of Greece, Spain and Portugal who have privileged relations with Latin-America and Arabia countries could be a unique opportunity to develop a new European strategy towards the Third World, in contractual terms. Finally, there are few, if any, arguments for protectionism that can stand up as long-term arguments. In Europe, most governmental interferences in the trade and industrial process have been ineffective. Some even suggest that we are in a period of slower growth in world trade, in production and in productivity as a result of the inefficiencies of protectionist industrial policies. To make plausible the interest of a drastic change in the European attitude, it would be necessary to develop arguments about the efficiency of new tools of protectionism. A reference to the Japanese situation which we are unable (and probably unwilling) to achieve for social, cultural and political reasons, is not sufficient.

To conclude, instead of a drastic shift towards more protectionism, it is necessary to maintain our decentralized and open economic system founded on the willingness to take risks, to encourage mobility of resources and creativity. This does not exclude occasional and temporary protection, but based on selective and widely debated arguments. This also implies a stronger solidarity between member states expressed in more powerful common social and regional policies.

Footnotes

[1]See L. Franko, Industrial policies in Western Europe. *The World Economy*, n°1, January 1979.

[2]See J. Sachs, Stabilization policies in the world economy. *American Economic Review*, May 1982.

[3]See M. Bruno, Raw materials, profits and the productivity slowdown. NBER Working Paper n°660R, Cambridge, 1981.

[4]J. Lesourne, Industry and the next decade, in *International Symposium on Industrial Policies for the 80's*. The Spanish Ministry of Industry and Trade, Madrid, 1982.

[5]For an overall analysis, see Commission of the European Communities, *Competitiveness of European Community Industry*. Document of the Commission's Services, Brussels, 5 March 1982.

[6]For the case of the United Kingdom see R. Bacon and W. Eltis,

Britain's Economic Problem : Too Few Producers (London, McMillan, 1976). See also the very stimulating paper of A. Singh, U.K. industry and the world economy : a case of de-industrialisation ? in A. Jacquemin and H. de Jong, *Welfare Aspects of Industrial Markets* (Leiden, Nijhoff, 1977), who shows the role of the world market conditions. For a confirmation of Kaldor's hypothesis that there is a close relationship between the rate of growth of a country's GDP and the growth of its manufacturing sector, see T.F. Cripps and R.J. Tarling, *Growth in Advanced Capitalist Economies* (London, Cambridge University Press, 1974), who have analysed the growth process in advanced industrial countries during 1950-1970.

[7]See for example R. Linda in *Regulating the Behaviour of Monopolies and Dominant Undertakings in Community Law.* Collège d'Europe (Bruges, de Tempel, 1977), p.62, where it is calculated that in 53% of the 301 European markets that were analysed the principal company controlled 40% of its national market.

[8]For a general analysis of these different aspects, see A. Jacquemin and H. de Jong, *European Industrial Organisation* (London, McMillan, 1977).

[9]L. Stoleru, *L'impératif industriel* (Paris, Seuil, 1969), p.186.

[10]R. Toulemon and J. Flory, *Une politique industrielle pour l'Europe* (Paris, PUF, 1974), p.17.

[11]A. Jacquemin, *Economie industrielle européenne* (Paris, Dunod, 1979), p. 324; H. Bauwens in Cepess, *Politique industrielle* (Bruxelles, 1974), p.7.

[12]H. de L'Estoile, Les objectifs actuels de la politique industrielle en France in *Politique industrielle et stratégies d'entreprises* (Paris, Institut de l'Entreprise, Masson, 1977), pp.124-125.

[13]J. Meade, *The Just Economy* (London, Allen and Unwin, 1976), chap.VIII.

[14]For a recent analysis, see D. Carlton, The disruptive effect of inflation on the organization of markets. Mimeo, NBER, Washington D.C., 1981.

[15]In the Theory of Games, this view is well-established for the case of the "prisoner's dilemma". In the well-known two-person nonzero-sum non-cooperative game which is ubiquitous in the economy, it is shown that, contrary to the doctrines of liberal economics, the group interest is not furthered by the independent pursuit of individual interests. The "Pareto-better" joint maximum position is forcibly repelled by the players because of the dominant character of their individual strategies. The situation is still more complex if the joint maximum position is not "Pareto-improving" because a player would worsen his position by such a change. Then the bigger utility total must be shared out by a suitable international distribution to make the players better off than they would have been.

[16]See S. Holland, Europe's new public enterprises in R. Vernon (ed), *Big Business and the State, Changing Relations in Western Europe* (London, McMillan, 1974), p.41.

[17]E. Malinvaud, Les perspectives de la croissance française in *Colloque sur le redéploiement industriel* (Paris, La Documentation Française, 1975), p.102.

[18]See A. Jacquemin, *Op. Cit.*, p.191 et seq. for a survey.

[19]For details, see *The Fifteenth General Report on the Activities of the European Communities*. Brussels, 1982, pp.204-212.

[20]EEC Commission, *Programme of the Commission for 1977* (Brussels, February 1977).

[21]EEC Commission, *Sixth Report on Competition Policy* (Brussels, April 1977).

[22]EEC Commission, *Tenth General Report on the Activities of the Community* (Brussels, 1977).

[23]EEC Commission, *Programme of the Commission for the Year 1977* (Brussels, 1977).

[24]EEC Commission, *Fourth Medium-term Economic Programme : Concerning the Period 1976-1980*. COM(76)530 Final (Brussels, 5 October 1976).

[25]Official Journal of the European Communities, n°L101,25, April 1977.

[26]E. Davignon, Ebauche d'une stratégie européenne pour surmonter la crise industrielle. *Revue de la Société d'Etudes et d'Expansion*, n°273 (September 1977).

[27]Commission of the European Communities, *A Community Strategy to Develop Europe's Industry*. COM(81)639 (Brussels, 23 October 1981).

[28]This system enables any user with access to a suitable terminal linked to the telephone network to interrogate interconnected data bank. The tariff for the service is based not on distance but on interrogation time.

[29]See W. Haeger, Industrial policy in an enlarged community in J. Girão (ed), *Southern Europe and the Enlargement of the EEC*. Economia, Lisboa, 1982; J.M. Jeanneney, *Pour un nouveau protectionisme* (Paris, Seuil, 1978).

[30]See B. Balassa, Prospects for trade in manufactured goods between industrial and developing countries, 1978-1990. *Journal of Policy Modeling*, n°2, 1980.

PART THREE

FISCAL POLICY

A. R. Prest

I Theoretical Background

We shall interpret the words "fiscal policy" as covering the various ways in which public finances have been or will be affected by the evolution of the EC, both in terms of the development of the EC budget itself and also that of member country finances. Whilst our main concern will be the examination of those items of revenue and expenditure which enter into budgets in an explicit manner we shall also have a little to say about some which are of an implicit character.

There is a very large range of literature which is relevant to our subject. First of all comes the subject of the scope and method of the public sector in a single country considered on its own: what functions should be undertaken by the public sector, how should they be financed, how should they be divided between upper and lower tiers of government, what different conclusions apply in the case of federal compared to unitary government structures and so on.

When more than one country is considered, attention has to be paid to the resource and equity effects of public finance measures which influence flows of goods, services and factors across frontiers. Tariffs, excise or sales taxes or (in some circumstances) corporation taxes may distort trade patterns. Whilst taxes on income are the principal deterrent to factor flows, taxes on goods which work themselves out through reductions in income rather than increases in prices may have non-trivial effects. And some expenditure policies such as subsidies to domestic production or public purchasing policy may also affect trade or factor flows. Equity aspects arise in that the precise tax and expenditure measures adopted may have effects on the distribution of income between individuals, countries or regional areas.

Another category of complications arises when countries link together but the relationship falls short of a full merger. Free trade areas, customs unions, common markets, monetary unions all have their own particular features. The abolition of tariffs between member countries, the adoption

Coffey, P. (ed.): Main Economic Policy Areas of the EEC
© 1983. Martinus Nijhoff Publishers, The Hague / Boston / London
ISBN 90-247-2793-6.

of a common external tariff, the substitution of a common monetary unit for individual country ones and the locking together of exchange rates pose differing questions for fiscal policy. It should be emphasised that there is an enormous amount of variety in these arrangements with, for instance, historical examples of customs unions without labour mobility (the ex-British Caribbean) and labour mobility without a customs union (U.K. and Ireland for the fifty years up to 1973).

Such are the areas of economic literature potentially relevant for our purposes. To see what is actually relevant, we must now sketch in some of the salient features of the EC.

The EC does not fit easily into any of the traditional classifications used by economists. It is clearly something more than just a customs union in that it does have a layer of government separate from national governments and, moreover, with its own sources of finance. It is also clearly marked off, for the same reason, from international organisations financed by subscriptions from member governments. On the other hand, it lacks many of the attributes of weak federations, let alone strong ones or unitary states. The total EC budget is miniscule compared to the national budgets or G.D.P. of member countries. And within this total there is a very heavy concentration on one object of importance, agriculture. It is also much more a matter of revenue sources and expenditure functions being prised from the grasp of member countries rather than of them trickling down from upper to lower government levels. There is no common monetary system; exchange rates are linked through the European Monetary System (E.M.S.) but scarcely locked for all time; although tariffs have gone for intra-Community trade, there are still a number of not inconsiderable impediments of one sort or another, including fiscal frontiers; nor is the freedom of factors to move from country to country anything like complete.

So we have an unconventional beast which does not fit easily into any of the normal categories. It follows that it is selected parts of economic theory rather than whole categories which are relevant to EC fiscal matters. We shall in fact single out three topics for detailed discussion: tax and expenditure harmonisation to facilitate trade flows; tax and expenditure harmonisation to facilitate capital flows; and budgetary matters. As the first two received attention and emphasis before the last one we shall follow that historical sequence in our discussion even though simple logic might suggest the converse.

The obvious starting point must be the consideration of what is meant in broad general terms by harmonisation in the fiscal area, without pretending in any way that this rather elusive concept has the same meaning in other contexts.

The Neumark Report (<u>Report of Fiscal and Financial Committee</u>, 1963, p188) had this to say:

'What then is the essential aim of tax harmonisation? It is to encourage the interplay of competition in such a way that integration and economic growth of the six countries may be achieved simultaneously and gradually. It is not a problem of the structure of the tax systems but a question of the effects and incidence of taxation operated in each country on the processes of integration and economic growth.'

This quotation gets near to the heart of the matter but so many different ideas are to be found on the subject that it is worth further definition.

A low level meaning would be to identify harmonisation with "co-ordination". This could in turn be interpreted to be some process of consultation between member countries or, possibly, loose agreements between them to levy taxes on a similar sort of base or at similar sorts of rates. A high-level meaning would be "standardisation" implying that the base and rates of any given tax should be identical in all member countries, the EC having the deciding voice in the precise definition of base and rates. It seems fair to say that in practice tax-structure or tax-rate harmonisation has come to mean something in between these limits.

Another sense in which harmonisation can be said to mean something between these limiting cases of co-ordination and standardisation is that the process by which agreement is reached is one in which the Commission plays an active but not an overwhelming role; it cannot be said that member country or Commission wishes alone prevail. Another way of looking at the subject is to think of two extreme cases: first, where individual country taxes and subsidies impede the free flow of trade across frontiers; and, second, where there is a single unified market inside one country. Harmonisation certainly means tax arrangements which will not impede trade flows; on the other hand, it does not mean an identical tax base and rate structure in each and every country. Thus harmonisation falls short of any idealised notion of a single unified market but not very short, if at all, of the situation in some countries where competition thrives vigorously even though tax bases and rates differ from area to area within them.

U.S. State sales taxes are an obvious example. There is no concerted attempt at a standardised pattern of coverage or rates but nonetheless there is no impediment to trade between states. But it should be clearly understood that this benign state of affairs depends on two well-understood rules of the game: first, rate divergences are generally not enormous (and, if by mischance they are so in isolated cases, the system does creak); and secondly, no one loses too much sleep about minor infringements such as buying liquor in a low tax area for consumption in a high tax one.

Another analogy is to be found in the specification of safety standards for cars in the EC. It is not necessary to stipulate that the safety tests should be identical in every member country provided that they are sufficiently alike to make it possible for each country to accept a car certified as having passed the safety test applied in another member country. In a very similar way, fiscal arrangements do not need to be identical but must have a certain degree of conformity.

We must now apply these general principles of tax harmonisation to trade flows i.e. we need to know which types of tax will interfere and not interfere with the free flow of trade between countries. This is mainly a matter of indirect taxes - and given the abolition of intra-Community tariffs that in turn means sales taxes and excise taxes - but insofar as a corporation tax is deemed to be passed forward we then have the equivalent of a form of sales tax. So we must have that possibility in mind too. We shall draw our main conclusions from the examination of value added tax principles and will subsequently ask what differences rise in the case of excise taxes.

It is a well-known piece of economic theory (Musgrave, 1969, ch.11) that a sales tax levied on a destination basis will not in general upset comparative costs. One has to be careful about specifying the argument precisely e.g. what is the relevant revenue alternative or how is additional revenue spent. One must also recognise that the story depends on whether one assumes a uniform or differentiated sales tax; and on whether one assumes forward or backward shifting and fixed or flexible exchange rates. Nevertheless, the broad result is that the relative ability of one country to compete with another will be unaffected by a destination arrangement which treats imported and home-produced goods alike.

With origin taxes, there are no problems if there is a single tax rate in a country A applying to all goods and services and also a single uniform tax rate in B. The two tax rates do not have to be the same, provided that there is sufficient flexibility of domestic wage rates and/or exchange rates to secure balance of payments equilibrium. In fact, one can go further still and show that there can be differential rates of origin tax in a country without impeding trade provided that these differentials are exactly mirrored in other countries (Fratianni and Christie, 1981). so there are some origin-base cases where trading conditions remain unaffected, though once again the arguments have to be specified very carefully (see e.g. J. Whalley, 1979, for the proposition that a balanced trade position is a necessary condition).

However, the origin principle no longer qualifies for this accolade if the ratio of tax rates in one country departs form that in another e.g. country A may tax all its products except one at a rate of x% and country B may tax all its products at y%, but the one black sheep immediately upsets comparative advantages.

The dilemma which arises, and to which we shall return more than once, is that there are circumstances in which it may be thought that the origin principle has advantages over the destination principle, especially where fiscal frontiers do not exist between countries or where it is thought desirable to abolish them. But origin principles incorporating differing ratios of tax rates between goods x and y in countries A and B will upset trade flows. So it would seem that one <u>either</u> has to give up the aim of abolishing fiscal frontiers <u>or</u> ensure that origin taxes conform to these rules. The first may be undesirable; the second infeasible.

Much the same problem as with sales taxes arises with excise taxes imposed at the stage of manufacture or importation. But two particular points should be noted about excise taxes. The first is that failure to tax at the first stage cannot be compensated by higher liability to tax at a later stage in the production and distribution process, as with a multi-stage-sales tax. The second is that differences in country excise tax rates in respect of the traditional items of taxation (alcohol, tobacco, petrol) are likely to be far greater than those arising with single or multiple stage sales taxes. This raises many awkward problems to which we return later.

Finally, there is an equity issue to be considered as well as resource allocation matters. A case can be made on equity grounds for applying either the destination or the origin principle to commodity taxes. To some extent this is a matter of one's view of the incidence process. But on the conventional assumption that a large proportion of the tax is passed forward, it would seem easier to justify the destination principle in that the tax burden will then fall on domestic rather than foreign consumers; and this might be thought to be more defensible.

What can be said about harmonisation principles in the context of factor flows? Obviously, we must look at capital flows first but we shall have a little to say on labour movements later. Our prime consideration must be taxes imposed on incomes but we should not forget that commodity taxes impinging on factors may also alter the relative gross returns available in different countries and so, potentially, factor flows.

The main tax relevant to capital flows is corporation tax though subsidiary or related taxes such as withholding taxes on dividends also have to be allowed for. Thinking first of all of corporation tax inside any one country, there are a number of standard issues of resource allocation and equity. One is the correct measurement of profits involving the choice of appropriate depreciation rules, inventory accounting and the like, all rendered far more complex in an age of inflation. Another is the precise relation between the taxation of profits at the corporation level and that of dividends in the hands of shareholders with the choice between an entirely separate system of taxation and one which is integrated in one way or another. These issues are discussed at length in Prest and Barr (1979, chs. 16 and 17) and I shall not repeat the arguments in detail. To illustrate, it can be maintained that the separate system has both resource allocation and equity disadvantages in that the overall tax level on undistributed profits is less than that on those distributed and so retentions are encouraged, thereby weakening capital markets and enabling richer shareholders to shelter behind the corporate tax rate rather than be exposed to higher marginal rates of personal income tax.

If one now moves to the international setting, there are a number of general resource allocation points to consider first. It has long been accepted that capital flowing across national frontiers should not be subjected to the full weight of taxation in both the country of source of profits and in that of residence of recipients. The two principal ways of avoiding such an outcome are the capital export neutrality principle (i.e. where the origin country taxes profits and the residence country also taxes profits but allows relief against the former) and the capital import neutrality principle (i.e. where only the origin country taxes profits). Either of these principles can operate is such a way as to offer no impediment to capital flows but there are circumstances in which both of them fall short in this regard. On the whole, it seems reasonable to think of the first principle as being more likely to satisfy neutrality requirements than the second; but the issue is a contested one. Insofar as the capital export neutrality principle is endorsed there is a further choice to make. One can either grant a credit of foreign taxes against home taxes or allow foreign taxes as a deduction against taxable profits in the home country. From an international viewpoint, i.e. that of not impeding capital flows in search of the highest pre-tax rate of profit, the former is correct; but from a purely national viewpoint, one can argue that the deduction principle satisfies the criterion that the same amount of tax should be paid on the same level of profits receivable in a country.

Many other problems also arise in this area. If an investor in a bloc of countries has the same tax treatment wherever he invests within that bloc but does not have the same treatment if he invests outside, capital flows may be diverted in such a way as to diminish efficiency from an international standpoint (Bird and Sato, 1976, p448). Nor is it sufficient to confine one's attention to the taxation of corporate profits in the relevant countries without also looking at the tax treatment of dividends, interest and royalties across frontiers.

So far we have confined ourselves largely to efficiency matters in respect of transfrontier capital flows and their taxation. But there are also important equity considerations. Transfer pricing, other than at arm's length, between the subsidiaries of a multinational enterprise will alter the distribution of profits between countries. So will some systems of integration between corporate profits and shareholder dividend taxation.[1]

There are also other issues such as whether the tax treatment of foreigners should be identical with that of nationals in a country (Musgrave, 1969 p258).

As in the case of product taxes we face an awkward dilemma. It is usually argued that separate taxes are inferior to an integrated corporate profits and dividends tax system from the viewpoint of capital market functioning; on the other hand, it is not difficult to demonstrate, as we shall see later, that an integrated system may impede transnational capital flows more than a separate system. So one has a very awkward choice. We shall come later to the EC proposals for avoiding the horns of this dilemma but we can note here and now that any idea of keeping a separate system in some countries and an integrated system elsewhere would not be satisfactory on the international, quite apart from the national, plane. [2]

We said earlier that we should have a little to say about tax impediments to labour migration. There are two main points here. Insofar as workers cross frontiers on a regular basis, liability to tax in the country of work will need to be offset in some way against tax liability in country of residence. Otherwise, a man who earned a given income living and working in country A would be differentially treated compared to a man earning the same income but working in country B and living in country A. this would clearly flout the usually accepted principles of horizontal equity and in addition could upset labour flows across frontiers though one then rapidly finds oneself in the shifting sands of discussing the optimal level of such frontier flows. Similar problems also arise with guest workers spending longer periods of time working in another country but the likelihood of liability to tax in the country of origin is then much reduced.

Another labour migration issue relates to social security. Whether one is thinking of daily migration or long-term residence in another country, there is obviously a problem of how far social security contributions paid abroad will secure benefits at home, especially pension benefits after retirement. There is clearly a need for some sort of international crediting system in this regard.

We now turn to budgetary principles. It must be emphasised from the beginning that we cannot hope to find precise guidance from standard economic literature on budgeting in that it is typically concerned with the relevant principles in a single country, whether of a federal or unitary nature, rather than a supra-national authority. So we must be prepared for some adaptation of the usual criteria.

With regard to the expenditure functions appropriate to the EC, the general principles are much the same as with the division between central and local government. Where proximity to the electorate is important, the lower down the expenditure responsibility the better. Where there are marked economies of scale or opportunity for internalisation of externalities, the reverse holds. Plausible cases can also be made for expenditure at EC level to compensate for economic changes due to the operations of the EC or for some degree of co-ordination in running down the scale of activity in declining industries or regions.

In allocating financial resources to the EC level, the principal question is the degree of independence which is to be given to it, in a very similar way to that in which local authorities can be said to be more independent of central government, the less they are reliant on grants from it. It should be noted that no question need arise of tax <u>collection</u> at EC level as distinct from tax <u>allocation</u>, provided that a reasonably comparable basis for allocation can be devised in each member country.

The links betwen revenue and expenditure are the next topic. There are two opposing principles here: one is that a specific tax source should be made available for a specific form of expenditure; the alternative is the concept of a common pool of funds. The former principle would tend to be associated with the notion of benefit or <u>juste</u> <u>retour</u>; the latter with ability to pay. And either of these notions could be thought of in the context of a Community stratified by income levels or geographical area.

Another decision to be taken is whether deficit financing should be allowable at the EC level. This is partly a matter of whether one upholds a rigid balanced budget rule as a matter of principle (Brennan and Buchanan, 1980) on economic and/or political grounds; and partly a matter of whether, even if the imbalance principle is accepted, there is a case for deficit financing at EC as distinct from the national level. This depends on whether one thinks that over time even if not at present the business cycles in the member states are likely to converge sufficiently to make EC macro-economic intervention desirable or sensible.

Yet another matter of decision is the process for changing the revenue or expenditure content of the EC budget. Some authorities (Brennan and Buchanan, 1980) would argue strongly for imposing strict constitutional limits on the power of legislatures to raise tax rates, tax revenues etc. This is clearly a very important and highly contentious subject.

Once all these decisions of fundamental principle are taken there are many practical details of budgeting which have to be settled. I have classified these elsewhere (Prest, 1975) under four headings - budget formulation (including such items as how one treats expenditure implications for succeeding years), authorisation (the process of gaining legislative approval), implementation (the process of disbursing funds on agreed items of expenditure) and post mortem (subsequent examination of budgeting for conformity with the law, accounting and economic principles etc). Obviously no budget system will be fully effective if any one of these four stages is neglected.

We have discussed tax harmonisation and budgetary principles under two separate headings. But it should be noted that the subjects may be connected. In the case of the EC, harmonisation of the value added tax base and rates is highly relevant to the free flow of goods between countries, most especially if the removal of fiscal frontiers dictates a move to the origin system for intra-community trade. On the other hand, one of the sources of own revenue for the EC is a value added tax levy in each country. This cannot possibly work equitably unless there is a commonly agreed base (as distinct from rates) for VAT in each country. So although the two topics of tax harmonisation and budgetary principles were treated separately for expository purposes, it should not be thought that there are no links between them.

II The EC Record

The first subject is obviously the abolition of internal tariffs within the EC and the imposition of the common external tariff with respect to the rest of the world. This programme was carried through without any major hitches although there are to this day temporary periods during which tariff walls are effectively reinstated by one means or another and also a number of non-tariff walls which have received considerable attention. However, we shall not have anything more to say about this subject here as it has been dealt with on a number of occasions by other people (e.g. Swann, 1978).

We must spend a good deal more time on the extent to which domestic indirect taxes have been aligned over the years. The starting point for this process was Article 99 of the Treaty of Rome which explicitly provided for harmonisation in the indirect taxation field. But the first substantial step was the Neumark Report (1963) which set out the various possible alternatives and the advantages and disadvantages of each. On the basis of this report it was decided to aim at a common system of value added taxation throughout the Community and for the original six members this came into operation reasonably speedily. It has also been an obligation on all new members joining the Community at a later date to adopt VAT.

The main features of VAT as it developed over the 1960s and the early 1970s were that the tax was based on the destination rather than the origin principle; full credit was allowed for investment expenditure; the general method by which tax was assessed was the tax from tax procedure, depending on invoices issued by firms, rather than on an accounts basis; although the Neumark Commmittee was somewhat apprehensive about the speed with which the retail sector could be covered by such a tax, this in fact rapidly became an accepted part of the system; and finally, a number of goods and services were exempt (and so outside the scope of the tax) and zero rating applied in some other cases. The distinction between exemption and zero rating is by now very well known but essentially it means that with exemption any particular stage of production or distribution is not taxed on its outputs but in turn gets no credit for any VAT on its inputs; whereas with zero rating no tax is payable on output but credit is given in respect of VAT paid on inputs.

The cohesiveness throughout the Community is due to a number of Directives and in particular the Sixth Directive of 1977. The general aim of this Directive was that of structural harmonisation in the sense of trying to establish a common list of taxable activities and a common list of exemptions including a lower limit of transactions below which exemption was allowed. Common definitions were adopted for taxable persons and taxable supplies and so on.

The general intention was that the Sixth Directive should provide a common base so that there could be an equitable imposition of the VAT levy for budget purposes; and so there was no necessity at all to introduce a common set of tax

Table 1

VAT Rates (%) July 1982

Country	Standard	Reduced	Increased
Belgium	17	6	25
Denmark	22	-	-
France	18.6	5.5,7	33.3
Ireland	30	o,18	-
Italy	15	2,8	18,35
Luxembourg	10	2,5	-
Netherlands	18	4	-
U.K.	15	0	-
W.Germany	13	6.5	-

Source: Bulletin of the EC Supplement 1/80 1980 plus information from H.M.Customs and Excise on later changes.

Notes: 1. Greece has not yet introduced VAT.
2. Proposals were made in August 1982 for increasing the rates of tax in Italy (e.g. 35% to 38%).

rates at that stage. The present structure of tax rates in the Community is shown above in Table 1.

It can be seem that the rate structure still differs considerably in the Community, there being an enormous contrast between the countries with high and low rates (e.g. Italy maximum rate 35% and W. Germany maximum rate 13%); and another enormous contrast between countries with a small number of rates and those with a large number (e.g. Denmark with 1 rate and Italy with 5).

One further point should be noted about the common structure identified in the Sixth Directive. This structure does not necessarily apply in any single country in the Community in that derogations are permitted in respect of practices already established by the member countries. Thus, for instance, zero rating is more frequent in the U.K. than elsewhere and the small business exemption limit is higher but these practices were already established before the Sixth Directive and therefore they are allowed to continue, although formally only on a temporary basis. The implication of these departures from the structure set out in the Sixth Directive is that the Community VAT levy is not specifically tied in to actual value added tax coverage in any given country but rather to the notional structure set out in the Sixth Directive. So therefore the basis for imposing the levy is to calculate what value added in the country would be if the Sixth Directive applied in full as distinct form what any particular country VAT system in fact covers.

Although the Community can claim to have accomplished a great deal on the VAT front, the same is not true with respect to excise taxes. Despite a number of attempts by the Commission, notably one in 1972, to establish some basis or other for harmonisation of excise taxes the fact remains that extremely little has been accomplished in this field. the only point worth recording is that duties on cigarettes have been partly harmonised by introducing a new structure of excise taxes partly on a specific and partly on an *ad valorem* basis, with limits on the ratio of one component to the other.

With corporation tax there have been a number of developments. First of all, the Neumark Committee (1963) suggested a split rate system of tax arguing that the basis for a common structure was to be found in Article 100 of the Treaty of Rome. It was perhaps natural at the time that the Committee should look on the example of W. Germany as being the most appropriate one for the Community to follow. However, the decision of France in the 1960s not to adopt a split rate system but to go for an imputation system led to another report on corporation tax in the Community (Van den Tempel 1970). In this report it was suggested that the appropriate base was the separate system as practised in Holland and the United States; this again was not surprising given the source of the report. This recommendation too did not find favour with the EC and the first Draft Directive on the subject published in 1975 took a very different route.

There were four main proposals in this Directive. First of all, it was suggested that the corporation tax rate for all member countries should lie within the limits of 45% and 55%. Secondly, it was proposed that on French lines an imputation credit against income tax payable on dividends should be allowed in respect of the underlying corporation tax. The imputation credit and the link to what is called in the United Kingdom a tax credit (i.e. a fraction of the cash dividend paid out) can be set out very simply algebraically.

Let a = Corporation Tax Rate
b = Imputation Credit Rate
c = Tax Credit Rate

$$\text{Then } c = \frac{a}{100-a} \times b$$

i.e. The rate of imputation credit equals the rate of tax credit if a = 50%.

The third component of the 1975 Draft Directive was that tax should be levied on companies where dividends have not been the occasion of any tax at the corporate level and that this rate of tax should match the credit allowed on the dividends against personal income tax. It was made clear that, where there is already a system of corporation tax payable in advance at the time when dividends are paid out, as in the U.K. and France, this provision would be superfluous; or to put the whole point another way round, the idea behind this provision was to extend the system operating in the United Kindom and France to all other Community members. A further point was that this tax would form the basis on which credits would be allowed against tax liabilities of dividend recipients anywhere inside the Community. The implication of this arrangement was that the country where the profits originated would collect corporation tax but not the sum allotted for tax credit purposes and, on the other hand, the country where the dividend recipient was resident would receive the tax credit plus any personal income tax. Alternatively, one might say that this method was conceived as a way of avoiding the impediment to capital flows which would otherwise arise with an imputation system of tax. Taking as an example a U.K. based company operating in Ireland and assuming that the same tax rates prevail for corporations and individuals in both countries then in the absence of the 1975 proposals one would find that there was a net deterrent to capital flows between the two countries in that the U.K. corporation operating in Ireland would pay more tax in toto the same level of profits than it would have done if those profits were generated within the United Kingdom. The full rate of Irish corporation tax would have to be paid on profits but any dividends paid out in the United Kingdom would attract United Kingdom advance corporation tax and there would be no mainstream corporation tax against which this advance payment could be debited. Under the new arrangement proposed in 1975 the Irish Government would get less revenue than previously, by virtue of losing the revenue payable as a tax credit to the U.K. The U.K. Government would get the same revenue as before in that it would still collect advance corporation tax in respect of dividends paid out but the U.K. company would be reimbursed for this payment by the tax credit from the Irish Government. So the overall position would be that the Irish Government would lose some revenue, the U.K. Government's position would be the same but the U.K. company would be better off than before and hence the previous impediment to capital flows betwen the two countries would, broadly speaking, disappear.

The fourth element of the 1975 proposals was that all corporations should impose a 25% withholding tax on dividends except in two cases, the first being where there was a distribution between a subsidiary and its parent within the Community and the second where the dividend was paid to a shareholder known to the tax authorities in the relevant country. By definition a withholding tax is ultimately recoverable but these two provisions were inserted to reduce the scale of the temporary withholding and subsequent recovery.

It has to be recorded that until now very little progress has been made in this field of harmonising corporation tax despite the 1975 Draft Directive. The current position with the structure of corporation tax and tax rates in the Community is set out in Table II and the disparities in structure and rates can easily be seen.

Two other aspects of corporation tax should be mentioned. The first is that the energies of the Community were concentrated for a long time on the harmonisation of

Table 2

Corporation Tax System, Rates etc. 1980

	System	Corporation Tax Rate %	Imputation Credit (if relevant)%
Belgium	Imputation	48	49.8
Denmark	Imputation	37	25.5
France	Imputation	50	50
Ireland	Imputation	45[1]	52.4[3]
Italy	Imputation	36.25[2]	58.6
Luxembourg	Separate	40	None
Netherlands	Separate	45	None
UK	Imputation	52	39.6[3]
W. Germany	(Imputation)[4]	56) 36)	100

Source: *Bulletin of the EC, Supplement* 1/80, 1980

Notes:
1. Ireland has lower rates in special areas.
2. Italy is sum of central and local rates (an increase in the central component was proposed in August 1982).
3. U.K., Ireland = imputation equivalent of tax credit.
4. German system is a two-rate imputation system.

corporation tax rates rather than the harmonisation of the base of the corporation tax in each country. In the course of the last two or three years attention has been directed to the latter aspect but so far there have been no pronouncements of any significance. The other point is that whereas the original six members of the Community apply what was called above the principle of capital import neutrality in respect of international flows of dividends and the like the three countries acceding to the Community in 1973 apply the principle of capital export neutrality. So far there have been no pronouncements from the taxation authorities of the Community in respect of the choice between these principles, though it should be noted that the competition authorities of the EC have declared in favour of the principle of capital import neutrality (*Bulletin Supplement* 1/80, 1980).

Progress in other taxation fields can be recorded very quickly. Four Directives were agreed some years ago relating to stamp duties in various forms and that does represent some achievement of harmonisation in that field. On the other hand the only sign of progress to date with respect to the taxation of migrant workers and the dangers of paying more tax than if they lived and worked in one country alone is a Draft Directive of 1979 which has not so far made any overt headway.

With respect to budgetary questions a good deal has happened in various ways. First of all, there has been some general tidying up of the elements covered by the general budget as distinct from subsidiary budgets over the years. There is now an agreement about the coverage of the accounts of such bodies as the European Coal and Steel Community and the European Investment Bank as distinct from the general budget. The size of the budget is of course extremely small when judged by the size of national budgets or of Community G.D.P. The current Community budget of some 22 b. ECU is considerably below 1% of Community G.N.P. (e.g. 0.80% is projected for 1983) whereas, for instance, the central government budget of the U.K. is approximately 35% of G.N.P.

It is well known that the expenditure composition of the EC budget is very heavily weighted towards agriculture, the usual proportion being somewhere around two-thirds of total expenditure. The other remaining items consist of regional and social expenditure (15% or so of the total) and then research and investment expenditure (2-3 per cent of the total), the remainder going in administration and various miscellaneous items.

The revenue side is very straightforward in that something like half the total revenue comes from the VAT levy on member countries. Present arrangements provide that the levy can go up to 1% and the likelihood is that the figure for 1983 will be something around 0.9%. The common external tariff provides something like one-third or more of total Community revenue and agricultural and sugar levies virtually all of the remainder i.e. some 14% or so . One particular point to note is that totally unlike central government budgets in the major federations of the world defence expenditure does not fall at all in the province of the EC budget.

The figures above relate to what might best be called the explicit budget of the Community in that they are the ones which appear in the official documents. But many people have pointed out that these figures are artificial, most especially because of the way the CAP works. The simplest way of stating the problem is to take an imaginary case where the United Kingdom imports wheat from N. America and French farmers are subsidised by the Community to sell wheat abroad. In such a case the levies on imported wheat would appear as part of the EC budget and similarly the subsidies on exported wheat. On the other hand, if the amount of wheat produced and consumed remains the same in Britain and France but Britain now imports wheat from France at EC prices rather than from N. America and the French no longer need to be subsidised to export their wheat there would be no entries in respect of such transactions in the Community budget. So depending on whether a given amount of wheat enters and leaves the EC or whether external trade is zero, the revenue and expenditure totals in the Community budget the revenue and expenditure totals in the Community budget are affected; and clearly the result is highly arbitrary. But it is easier to state the problem than to find a solution. Various people have put forward differing estimates of the level of these implicit taxes and subsidies (Pearce, 1981 for a description of of these different approaches) but none of them should be regarded as more than a rough attempt to correct for an anomalous situation.

A major topic which has received attention in the Community on many occasions is the distribution of Community revenues and expenditures between different countries. There are a number of major difficulties here in that, first of all, the inclusion or exclusion of implicit revenues and expenditures alters the picture; the attribution of import levies or customs duties to countries whose ports act as entrepots for onward movement of goods inside the Community poses a number of severe problems: and further difficulties arise with the attribution of monetary compensation amounts (Pearce, 1981). But for what they are worth the figures are reproduced below in Table 3.

Table 3
Distribution of EC Revenues and Expenditures by Countries 1979 (M. ECU)

	Revenue From	Expenditure In
W. Germany	4407	2753
France	2887	2649
Italy	1793	2166
Netherlands	1344	1547
Belgium	967	843
Luxembourg	19	15
U.K.	2514	1541
Ireland	105	629
Denmark	337	704
Total	14372	12847

Source: Eurostat Review 1970-1978, Statistical Office of European Communities, 1981.

Notes:
1. Expenditures are adjusted for monetary compensation amounts.
2. Some common items of expenditures are not allocated between countries.

One other point should be made about the revenue side of the Community budget; borrowing is permissible in respect of some European Coal and Steel Community and European Investment Bank expenditure but not for normal current account expenditure.

There is now a well established set of budgetary procedures (Wallace, 1980). Summarising very briefly, the including the Commission, the Council of Ministers, the European Parliament and the Court of Auditors. The powers of these different organisations are very different and are not uniform with respect to different types of expenditure in that the European Parliament can suggest amendments to certain types of expenditures but for the so called obligatory expenditures (including the major part of agricultural expenditure) the Parliament can only reject the budget as a whole as distinct from amending it.

The annual budgetary cycle is as follows:

April	Initial discussion by Council on the basis of a paper from the Commission
June	Preliminary budget drafted by Commission
July	Council discusses draft budget
October	Parliament amends draft budget
November	Council considers amendments
December	Parliament accepts or rejects the budget

III <u>Analysis of the Record</u>

We shall analyse the historical record in the Community starting with measures for tax harmonisation and subsequently coming to the budget.

If we look first of all at the progress of VAT the EC can take a reasonable pride in it. It should be remembered that the Neumark Committee (1963) was dubious about the extension of VAT to the retail sector and this in fact was achieved much more easily than might have been expected. At the same time there are plenty of ways in which the existing structure is imperfect, let alone the many steps which lie ahead in the Community's programme. Imperfections abound in a number of ways: derogations from the structure laid down in the Sixth Directive which are supposed to be temporary but clearly will be there for a long time to come; and little progress on a number of matters such as, for instance, the 1978 proposed harmonisation of VAT in relation to works of art, antiques and used goods. There are also reasons for thinking that VAT avoidance and evasion differ quite considerably between countries. And in so far as the ultimate goal is harmonisation of rates, with the idea of moving over to the origin system of VAT for intra-Community trade and the abolition of fiscal frontiers within the community, there is clearly a very long way to go.

With regard to excises, as we saw earlier, very little has been done and this is not surprising. It was foreseen in the Neumark Report (1963) that this was likely to be a much more intractable area than that of general sales taxation, there being so many reasons of history and social policy why countries take different views about appropriate levels of taxation on wines, spirits, tobacco and petrol.

But to illustrate the very wide discrepancies which remain in this area we cannot do better than reproduce figures given by the Commission some two years ago on the relative rates of taxation in 1979.

Table 4

Excise Duty Applicable in each Member State as a Percentage of the Community Average (= 100) (1 July 1979)

	Cigarettes	Spirits	Wine	Beer	Petrol (high grade)	Gas Oil
	(Community Average = 100)					
Belgium	86	62	69	46	99	85
Denmark	299	289	240	272	132	51
W. Germany	118	63	0	29	92	203
France	42	89	4	7	127	156
Ireland	74	147	218	289	76	72
Italy	57	18	0	34	140	27
Luxembourg	54	34	34	33	74	44
Netherlands	77	62	69	46	91	82
U.K.	92	136	265	144	68	180

Source: Bulletin of the EC, Supplement 1/80

It can be seen very readily from this table that the discrepancies in 1979 - and much the same applies today - were really enormous. Take, for instance, the difference between the rates of tax on cigarettes in France and Denmark or the difference between tax rates on wine in Italy and the United Kingdom. It will clearly be an heroic exercise even to think of reducing these differentials to a narrow band let alone concluding such an exercise successfully.

With regard to corporation taxes it was recorded earlier that there had been little effective progress in this field since the Draft Directive was published in 1975. This has partly been a matter of unwillingness to proceed further at Council level but also the European Parliament has raised objections (Chown and Hopper, 1982). One very simple way of summarising the position with respect to corporation tax is that between 1969 and 1978 there were five proposed Directives but only one actual Directive (which provided for mutual assistance on tax evasion). So there is a pretty long record of directives not getting beyond the proposed or draft stage in this field. With respect to base harmonisation for corporation tax a summary given of incentives to corporations in member states in 1980 gives us a simple picture of the very diverse pattern which prevails.

Table 5
Corporation Incentives in 1980

Incentive	Number of Countries
Accelerated depreciation	6
Deduction of investment costs from profits	3
Tax exemption from certain payments	4
Special exemptions for new firms	3
Unlimited loss carryovers for new firms	1
Exemptions on dividends on new shares	2
Manufacturing exports profits exemption	1
Tax exemptions on additions to reserves	3
Developing country concessions	1
Regional tax reductions	1
Tax incentives for labour force increases	1
New investment concessions	1

Source: *Bulletin of the EC, Supplement* 1/80

With regard to other tax aspects one might note that nothing effective has happened in respect of the social security problems mentioned above; also the Neumark Committee raised the point that wealth and inheritance taxation patterns in different countries might well affect migration between them but nothing whatever seems to have happened at EC level in this regard.

As for the achievements in the budgetary field the most important point is that the Community does now have its own sources of finance in the form of revenues from the common external tariff, agricultural import levies and the VAT contribution from each member country. It should also be emphasized that over the years the European Parliament has gained more powers in dealing with budgetary matters. A good example is to be found in the rough reception which it gave to the budget proposals in December 1979.

The main point to be emphasized about the budget is that there are serious problems about the future adequacy of financial resources to meet likely expenditures and that the composition of both the revenue side and the expenditure side, especially the latter, gives cause for a great deal of dissatisfaction. These two matters are not disconnected in that some of the expenditure reforms proposed would have automatically compensated for the inadequacies of revenue which have been perceived. Nevertheless, such a result is not automatic and one therefore has to treat these two points separately whilst recognising that there are links between them. We shall have more to say on this subject later but for the time being we should also note that the composition of the expenditure and revenue sides is also tied in to the distribution of these receipts and payments by income levels, countries, regions and so on.

The budgetary procedures which have evolved over the years have attracted a good deal of criticism most notably in the annual reports of the Court of Auditors (e.g. 1980, Official Journal 31 December 1981) which have pointed to defective accounting procedures, extravagance by officials, irregularities of budgetary control, inadequate supervision of bank balances and so on. So there is plenty of scope for criticism on these kinds of lines.

Perhaps a revealing light is shed on the budgetary position by referring to the well known report of the Macdougall Committee (Report, 1977) which made a large number of suggestions for the reform of the Community revenue and expenditure structure but some five years later there have been no perceptible effects flowing from these recommendations.

Another indication of the part played by the Community budget in its affairs today can be gauged from the quotation from Wallace (Wallace, 1980, p117).

'The budget has thus emerged as a consuming focus of political attention. It is not the only key issue, but it symbolises the central pre-occupation of member governments about the nature of the Community impact and poses awkward dilemmas about the distribution of authority between Community institutions and the member states.'

The overall judgement must be that the pace of Community development in the fiscal area, as in others, has perceptibly slackened in recent years. The impetus and drive towards tax harmonisation and towards any major budgetary reconstructions have clearly become much less evident. Nevertheless, one must recognise that the earlier achievement in removing intra-Community tariffs and in erecting a reasonably comparable VAT structure throughout all nine countries which have been members for a substantial period of time is a very real achievement. Perhaps the most appropriate comment is the famous one by Dr Johnson on a woman preaching: "like a dog's walking on his hinder legs. it is not well done; but you are surprised to find it done at all".

IV Proposals for the Future

It will be evident from what has been said that a number of proposals are already in the pipeline waiting to be adopted or modified or rejected; in other words, there is no shortage of business, whether one looks at the tax harmonisation side or at the budget side.

Looking first at tax harmonisation, there is a major issue with respect to VAT: whether the idea originally put forward in the Neumark Report (1963) of applying the restricted origin basis along with the abolition of fiscal frontiers should be adopted or not. One can see that there are compelling arguments for the abolition of fiscal frontiers; some of the relevant points have been summarised by Fratianni and Christie (1981). For instance, border formalities add to private costs and distort resource allocation e.g. by leading to the development of specialist firms which attract resources otherwise available for other purposes. It is also highly likely that fiscal frontiers reinforce the non-tariff barriers which are only too likely to flourish unless there is constant vigilance. Quite apart from such tangible economic drawbacks of fiscal frontiers there is the important emotional and psychological view that a United States of Europe cannot possibly be achieved whilst there is still a customs post on the Rhine.

These arguments should not be accepted too uncritically. there are some obvious reasons why it is convenient to have inspections of goods travelling by road, rail, air or water e.g. to enforce hygiene or safety standards, check on dangerous or illegal cargoes and so on. In addition, there are some customs posts which deal with both intra-Community and extra-Community trade and so can certainly not be abolished in their entirety. Nevertheless, when all this is said one can readily accept that there is a case for abolishing fiscal frontiers if possible.

But we now return to the dilemma pointed out earlier. The usual argument is that one cannot abolish fiscal frontiers unless one switches from the destination to the origin principle in that, by definition, if the frontier post has gone there is no method of applying tax at the point of importation into a country and so one is dependent upon applying it at the point of origin. On the other hand, the origin principle will lead to resource misallocation, trade impediments and so on unless the discrepancies in rates currently found in the EC member states are largely eliminated.

The conventional answer to this dilemma over the last twenty years or so has been to argue for the removal of these discrepancies. For instance, the Commission proposals published in March 1980 (Bulletin Supplement 1/80) envisage a two-tier rate of value added tax, one around 15-17% and the other around 3-5%, and the general objective should be to harmonise all VAT rates in the Community in this fashion. but the question is whether it is realistic to think that this can be done within foreseeable time. It is now a commonplace to declare that a snail's pace is extremely fast for EC developments but even by that standard it is hard to see that the rate structure set out in Table 1 above is likely to be harmonised within any reasonable period of time. Furthermore, it must be recollected that the present degree of structure harmonisation contains a large number of temporary exceptions but it would be astonishing if "temporary" did not in this context mean "long-lived".

It should also be remembered that the Community proposals envisage that the distribution of tax receipts would continue to be much the same as at present even if the restricted origin base had replaced the destination base. Thus if a commmodity is exported from France to Germany, then once the restricted origin base has come into operation the tax paid at the export stage in France would be deductible from any VAT payable subsequent to import into Germany. Therefore the net result, if nothing were done about it, would be that German tax receipts in respect of that transaction would be less than before and French tax receipts greater. More generally, the distribution of VAT between countries would change according to whether there was an excess of imports over exports and according to whether tax rates were higher in one country than in another. Obviously, if the country of export rather than that of import gets the first bite at tax receipts those countries with balance of payments surpluses on current account would tend to benefit at the expense of those countries with deficits. Similarly, to revert to the example above, the higher is the French level of VAT compared to the German level the larger the French bite of the cherry and the smaller the German one. To avoid this degree of redistribution of tax proceeds, which would clearly be unacceptable to loser countries, the Community has proposed a clearing house so that, to go back to the example above again, there would be a re-chanelling of tax receipts from France to Germany in such a way as to leave their tax revenues unchanged from what they were when the destination principle operated.

This seems a highly cumbersome method of approach and a much simpler one would seem to be as follows. In the case of transactions between registered traders by far the simplest thing would be to continue the destination principle so that exports from, say, France to Germany are free from tax at the point of export. It would not be feasible to collect tax at the point of import into Germany once fiscal frontiers had gone but the great advantage of the VAT mechanism is that it is immaterial whether the tax is collected at the first stage or at a later stage provided that there is no break in the chain of transactions. In other words, what would not be collected in tax at the point of import once physical frontiers had gone would be collected in tax at a later stage in the German production and distribution process. So one would end up with the retention of the destination principle for trade between registered suppliers and purchasers and without the problem of a clearing house to transfer tax revenues from one country to another. Obviously, various safeguards are necessary. For instance, agreement would be needed that

French exporters to Germany should supply, at any rate on a sample basis, the German tax authorities with the VAT numbers of the registered importers in Germany so that tax evasion could be minimised.

With regard to transactions between registered suppliers and unregistered pruchasers the obvious answer is to move to the origin principle in that case. In other words, the German tourist buying goods in France would not be freed from French VAT at the point of purchase but would not in turn pay German VAT on taking his goods into Germany. In so far as VAT rates differ between the two countries this does mean some redistribution of tax revenues but the amount involved would be of the second order of smalls. Exactly the same principle would have to apply, though the practical problems might well be greater, to mail order deliveries between registered suppliers and unregistered purchasers. There are other cases too which have to be considered in any comprehensive scheme. One could presumably neglect transactions between unregistered suppliers and unregistered purchasers; but some thought might have to be given to possible over-taxation in respect of sales from unregistered suppliers to registered purchasers when there may be a similar problem to that occuring inside a country A (registered) sells to B (unregistered) who in turn sells to C (registered). Matters are different again if the article in question is one (e.g. a used car or work of art) to which the normal tax from tax computation of liability does not apply.

This is a difficult area and it would be unwise to maintain that there is any straightforward solution which is completely without snags. Nevertheless, one must revert to the fact that United States sales taxes have worked reasonably well for many years despite the lack of frontier posts and despite the fact that the nominal taxes on usage in states where consumption but not purchase takes place have long been a dead letter. At least it would seem better to explore the kind of approach sketched out above, rather than beat one's head permanently against the solid brick wall of substantial national differences in VAT rates.

In case anyone should think that these ideas are brand new it is worth referring to a passage in the Neumark Report (1963, p68).

'In conclusion it does not seem out of the question that in a Value Added Tax system where rates are not yet unified, measures can be put in hand so as to avoid great distortion of competition and so as in principle to assign almost all the receipts to the consumer country. These measures would be the lighter the greater the rates of the different countries would tend to be unified.'

The argument sometimes made that a lot of the difficulty of switching from the destination to the origin principle would be avoided if there were sufficient flexbility of exchange rates does not in fact seem very promising. First, the argument only holds in its strict sense provided that the ratios of tax rates on goods x and y in country A are the same as the ratio of tax rates on goods x and y in country B. Second, the notion of exchange rate flexibility does not fit very easily into the context of the European Monetary System.

We now turn to excise taxes. These are in many ways much more difficult to cope with than VAT: firstly, because the rate structure varies even more than does that of VAT and, secondly, because the excise tax is normally imposed in one operation at an early stage in the production process and is not a fractional tax in the same way as VAT. Here again the Commission has argued that uniformity or near uniformity of rates was essential if the origin principles were to be adopted and the origin principle in turn was essential if fiscal frontiers were to be abolished. The answer once again seems to be that this is crying for the moon in the sense that there is little prospect this side of eternity of complete or even near-elimination of the differentials in the excise duties of the different countries. What might however be a possible alternative would be to place excise duties on an origin basis but to compensate by introducing special VAT rates (on a destination basis) on the standard items in question i.e. tobacco, alcohol, petrol. We should then have the following situation.

If, say, brandy is exported from France to Denmark excise taxes would be collected in France on Brandy but not in Denmark; on the other hand, before the brandy is sold in Denmark it is subject to value added tax in that country and that can be pitched at such a level as to mitigate very substantially any loss of tax which might otherwise occur in Denmark from excise duties currently being higher there than in France. Such would be the case for transactions between registered traders. In so far as sales take place across frontiers from traders to non-traders, whether by personal sale or by mail catalogue, then one would obviously not be able to levy the special value added tax in the country of consumption and therefore the sole tax would be the excise tax and VAT in the country where the sale takes place. The implication is that a certain amount of standardisation of excise taxes would be necessary in order to avoid a large scale temptation to ship goods across frontiers from registered sellers in low excise tax countries to non-registered purchasers in high excise tax countries. However, it would seem that the degree of standardisation involved might be less than that implied by the Commission's proposals as usually formulated. There are obvious problems such as net revenue transfers between countries but at least some sort of alternative on these lines is worth considering as a means of breaking what otherwise appears to be a rigid log jam.

Another alternative worth mentioning, though hardly one that is likely to be acceptable, is to think in terms of excise duties being imposed at Community level. After all, this is the relevant analogy from say, the United States where some main excise duties are imposed at federal level rather than at state level. But one must not be sanquine that any proposal of this kind would ever be likely to get off the ground given the lengthy history of and supportive interest in the variety of duties which one currently finds in Western Europe.

When we turn to corporation tax there is again plenty of unfinished business. Obviously, more work needs to be done on the proposals for base harmonisation particularly in respect of all those problems which arise under endemic inflationary conditions such as the appropriate level of depreciation allowances for capital goods, the adjustment of inventory values and changes in the real value of net monetary assets and liabilities. Without some systematization of these different tax allowances it is simply a hollow pretence to think that the conformity of nominal rates means conformity of effective rates of tax. at the same time there is a good case for going ahead with something like the 1975 Draft Directive in that the general proposition of a partial imputation system seems the most acceptable of the various possible alternatives. It might be added at this point that the case for full imputation of underlying corporaton tax against income tax on dividends would only be justifiable if one felt that no element of corporation tax is passed forward. In our present state of ignorance on these matters it is unwise to take a dogmatic attitude and a system of partial imputation may be the best alternative. There are many other alternatives which might be explored such as full integration, as recently proposed in Australia, meaning that the corporation is effectively treated like a partnership; various kinds of cash flow taxation and so on. Discussion of many of these alternatives is to be found in a Green Paper recently published by the U.K. Government. The other subject in this area is that of the choice between capital import and capital export neutrality. It might well be that any such decisions would provoke enormous squabbles and so it may be best to accept some sort of dual system without trying to push the boat too far in either direction.

One final point on corporation tax is that it is a delusion to think that it can be thought about on its own without discussing the taxation of unincorporated businesses and the taxation of capital gains. All these subjects are linked together and even though the main focus of attention may well be capital flows between corporate enterprises these other two aspects of the tax system need to be kept in view the whole time.

As for labour movement incentives, obviously it would make sense to implement the 1979 proposals for the treatment of migrants and there are still plenty of unresolved matters relating to the transferability of social security rights between countries.

We now come to the future of budgetary arrangements. We must first note that the present arrangements will need considerable revision if Portugal and Spain both join the Community in 1984. This is so for at least two reasons. one is that the problem of Mediterranean agricultural products (e.g. wine and olive oil) will be so much greater; in addition, Portugal's importing position is such that it would end up as a net contributor to the Community budget, which would hardly be appropriate for the poorest member of the Community. This need for review is quite separate from what people's views might be about the long drawn out controversy over the financial position of the United Kingdom in the EC.

There are two strategic alternatives in budgetary reform. One is to expand the revenue intake so as not just to allow the present expenditure level to continue but to supplement it with expenditure in other areas. The second is to keep something like the present revenue intake but to reduce the amount spent on agriculture so as to free funds for expenditure on other purposes. We shall now look at some of the detailed expenditure proposals which have been made and then come subsequently to revenue proposals germane to either of the two strategic alternatives.

A very large number of ideas have been put forward in respect of Community expenditure. First of all, many people have argued for cutting back the amount of expenditure devoted to agriculture or at the very least refusing to allow the present level of expenditure to increase even in nominal terms over the years. There is a large variety of ways in which such reforms could be implemented (e.g. one of those most frequently put forward is that the CAP should be taken out of the EC budget and financed by special national contributions) but it is beyond our scope to go into such matters in detail. It should be noted that many proposals of this sort would not just free funds for other purposes at Community level but would also be of direct assistance to those countries, such as the United kingdom, which are particularly hard hit by the CAP in its present form. With regard to expansion of other types of expenditure the MacDougall Committee made many different proposals related to possible hypotheses about the future development of the Community. Perhaps the most important ones related to expansion of regional and social expenditure which can be justified on many grounds such as the fact that Community development has led to progressive impoverishment of some regions or that it is highly appropriate for the Community to finance schemes designed to relieve unemployment in different ways. Some point can be given to these proposals by looking at the structure of the relative levels of income in different areas of the Community as shown in Table 6.

Table 6
Regional Differentials in the EC, 1978
(EC Average = 100)
Gross Value Added Per Head

(market price)

Country	All Regions	Richest Region	Poorest Region
Belgium	104	164	86
Denmark	114	-	-
W.Germany	118	191	101
France	110	160	87
Ireland	61	-	-
Italy	78	104	51
Luxembourg	115	-	-
Netherlands	103	128	85
U.K.	92	102	69

Source: *Regional Trends* H.M. Stationery Office, London, 1982

More refined measures of regional differentials could be made but that they exist on a dramatic scale can hardly be disputed.

Analogous kinds of additional responsiblity would be the expansion of the schemes for aiding infrastructure and industrial regeneration in different countries. Relatively small amounts are already spent for this purpose and it would be easy enough to direct these to those countries or those regions which were thought to be the most deserving of further expenditure.

Turning to revenue proposals, it has been suggested from time to time that the present country imbalance could be remedied by devices such as direct transfers from member state government to member state government on the lines of what now occurs between state governments in West Germany. but this would not seem to be very realistic. It has also been suggested that some of the tight limitations put on borrowing by the EC could be relaxed and this would seem to be sensible. Nevertheless, if revenue sources have to be expanded then in the last resort one must come down to some additional tax revenue. Probably the most acceptable is an expansion of the VAT base. This might take the simple form of increasing the limit beyond one per cent or it might take the more sophisticated form of a percentage which is variable depending on G.N.P. per head in a member state so that, for instance, the upper limit for W. Germany would be higher than the upper limit for Ireland. A whole variety of other suggestions have been made and many of these are catalogued in the 1978 Bulletin Supplement (Bulletin Supplement,8/78, 1978). The general conclusion was that one could think in terms of some sort of Community revenue source based on cigarettes or petrol but the authors were not exactly optimistic on the likelihood of either. Community revenues derived from energy or alcohol excise duties were thought to be even further away in the future. Basically this is all a matter of political attitudes and economists and economic commentators have little to contribute.

With regard to procedural aspects there are obviously a number of ways in which the deliberations of Parliament, the Council and the Commission might be better dovetailed than at present. (See The Times 24 July 1982 for an announcement that the 1983 budget would not be debated by Parliament until disagreements with the Council had been resolved.) The Court of Auditors has begun to produce extremely interesting reports but it is not yet apparent that they have had much effect on the bureaucracy. And clearly it is a highly unsatisfactory situation for Parliament to have much more limited powers over some forms of expenditure than others. Whilst recognising that the distinction between obligatory and non-obligatory expenditure is rooted in what is now history, that does not mean that the subject should be a closed book.

In conclusion, what one can readily say is that the fiscal aspects of the Community have been written about extensively and that there is no shortage of ideas or at least no shortage of old ideas. Perhaps two final points might be made. The first is that one does find a tendency to regard some of the earlier documents such as the Neumark Report as a bible containing eternal verities. It has to be remembered that that Report was written when only one country out of the original six had a VAT and that in a far from perfect form. So the whole perspective on matters such as VAT and excise taxes is today very different from what it was twenty years ago, when the Neumark Committee was making its deliberations (for a full account of developments in this area see Easson 1980, 1981). The very last point is that as one reads the literature and the statements and documents on EC fiscal matters one comes to the conclusion that nothing is ever decided except in the small hours of the day. This no doubt contributes to the feeling of innate superiority of those who survive such marathon exercises but whether it contributes to the wisdom of their decisions is an entirely different matter.

NOTES

[1] E.g. the split-rate system of corporation tax which prevailed in W. Germany before 1977 was held to bias the division of profits towards the U.S.A. rather than to W. Germany when U.S. corporations operated in both countries.

[2] E.g. if the U.K. has an imputation system of corporation tax and Ireland a separate one the corporation tax concessions made by the U.K. in respect of Irish subsidiaries operating there would tend to be negated by higher liabilities in Ireland.

BIBLIOGRAPHY

BIRD, R.M. and SATO, M., 'International Aspects of the Taxation of Corporations and Shareholders" I.M.F. Staff Papers, July 1975.

BRENNAN, G. and BUCHANAN, J.M., The Power to Tax: Analytical Foundations of a Fiscal Constitution, Cambridge University Press, Cambridge, 1980.

Bulletin of the EC Financing the Community Budget, Supplement 8/78, 1978.

Bulletin of the EC Report on the Scope for Convergence of Tax Systems in the Community, Supplement 1/80, March 1980.

BURKE, R.S., "Convergence of Tax Systems in the E.E.C." Fiscal Studies, November 1980.

CHOWN, J.F. and HOPPER, W., 'Company Tax Harmonisation in the European Economic Community' Intertax, 1982.

Corporation Tax, Cmnd 8456, H.M. Stationery Office, London, 1982.

Court of Auditors, Annual Report, EC, Brussels.

EASSON, A.J., Tax Law and Policy in the E.E.C., Sweet and Maxwell, London, 1980.

EASSON, A.J., "Tax Harmonisation in the E.E.C.: the Commission's Programme", British Tax Review, 1981 No. 6.

E.E.C. Budget, Select Committee of House of Lords on European Communities, HL 17, Session 1979/80, 9 June 1979, H.M. Stationery Office, London.

FRATIANNI, M. and CHRISTIE, H., "Abolishing Fiscal Frontiers within the E.E.C.", Public Finance, No. 3, 1981.

MUSGRAVE, R.A., Fiscal Systems, Yale University Press, New Haven, 1969.

PEARCE, Joan, The Common Agricultural Policy, Chatham House Papers 13, Royal Institute of International Affairs/Routledge Kegan Paul, London, 1981.

PREST, A.R., Public Finance in Developing Countries, Second Edition, Weidenfeld and Nicolson, London, 1975.

PREST, A.R. and BARR, N.A., Public Finance in Theory and Practice, Sixth Edition, Weidenfeld and Nicolson, London, 1979.

Report of the Fiscal and Financial Committee (Neumark Report), International Bureau of Fiscal Documentation, Amsterdam, 1963.

Report of Study Group on the Role of Public Finance in European Integration (MacDougall Committee), Vols. I and II, E.E.C., Brussels, 1977.

SNOY, B., Taxes on Direct Investment Income in the E.E.C., Praeger, New York, 1975.

SWANN, D., Economics of the Common Market, 4th Edition, Penguin, 1978.

VAN den TEMPEL, A.J., Company Tax and Income Tax in the European Comunities, E.E.C., Brussels, 1970.

WALLACE, Helen, Budgetary Politics: the Finances of the European Communities, Allen and Unwin, London, 1980.

WHALLEY, J., "Uniform Domestic Tax Rates, Trade Distortions and Economic Integration", Journal of Public Economics, April, 1979; see also further debate in Journal of Public Economics, December, 1981, pp 379-90.

PART FOUR

REGIONAL POLICY

Willem Molle

1. Introduction

Prosperity is spatially rather unequally distributed among the European regions; a regional policy is pursued to diminish the inequality, with the agencies of the European Community as well as the individual member states participating. We will first treat the subject in hand from a theoretical point of view and then characterise regional policy in general terms. Next, the most important regional problems of the European Community will be described. After that we come to the central element of this part of the book, namely, a brief discussion of the European Community's role in this regional policy.

Recently, quite drastic changes in some circumstances have made a new policy necessary. We shall therefore give some attention to the reorientation of policy. We shall conclude this part with some evaluating remarks about the current European regional policy.

2. Regional development; some theoretical aspects

Within every land there are regional differences in economic development among regions. These differences are more pronounced in some countries than in others. They are mostly measured by indicators such as the concentration of people and economic activities, the level of income per capital, the productivity by working person, and the availability and accessibility of environmental goods, cultural infrastructure, leisure activities, etc.

The theory of regional development indicates that these differences are the result not of incidental factors, but of a complex interplay of mutually dependent factors which in the past have always collectively determined the location of economic activities and people. Geographical

Coffey, P. (ed.): Main Economic Policy Areas of the EEC

ISBN 90-247-2793-6.

facts can be thought of, for instance the situation at the mouth of a rivier, or economic-technological factors that may have governed the cost relations of the production at various places, demographic factors that have influenced the volume and total growth of the population, etc. Such factors are changing constantly, but not necessarily towards a better equilibrium.

Regional equilibrium is a central element in literature, which of course mentions other element besides (Richardson, 1973, Paelinck and Nijkamp,1976). Most theories of regional development start from regions in a national setting.

Theory of regional development start with the classical school.

The basic assumptions of <u>(neo)classical</u> theory of regional development were: (a) free competition and entry, (b) full employment of factors of production, (c) full mobility of labour and capital, (d) equal technology (Paelinck and Nijkamp, 1976). Classical theory states that under these conditions the system will tend to equalise wages and rents across space, and tend to an equilibrium state. Now, in practice the conditions of neoclassical theory are never fulfilled and consequently the equalitarian end effect is not assured either. For one thing, labour and capital are not completely mobile in practice, so that factor incomes can become higher in one region than in another. Moreover, regions do not all start from an equilibrium position; historical and geographical factors have produced uneven situations, which in themselves put regions in different starting positions for future developments.

<u>International trade theory</u>, based on the Heckscher-Ohlin theorem, can be transposed to regions; it then states that a region will tend to specialise in the production and exportation of commodities for the production of which are needed large amounts of factors in relatively abundant supply there, and import commodities for the production of which it is at a comparative disadvantage. However, once more the theory is at odds with reality; the basic assumptions are not fulfilled in practice: transportation costs are not zero, production functions are not identical in different regions, there are economies and diseconomies of scale, and competition is not perfect (Vanhove and Klaassen, 1980).

Another theory is that of the <u>export base</u>, by which regional growth depends on the region's capacity to export products to other regions.

The more the region is specialised in products that are much in demand, the faster it grows. The lower income elasticity for its products, the slower growth. Differences in regional growth thus would spring from initial economic structures, which in turn can be attributed to historical and present-day comparative advantages (e.g. Andrews, 1963/56; Pfouts, 1957; Massey, 1973).

Quite contrary to the neoclassical theory, Myrdal (1957) in his cumulative causation theory stresses the initial disparities and the rigidity of the system, pointing out that under such conditions the free play of market forces will perforce lead to unbalanced regional growth because of backwash effects; for instance, labour will move to regions already far developed; capital will do the same, deserting regions with less chance of development. Thus, the latter regions will have become even less attractive in the next period. The author did not perceive merely negative effects, recognising indeed the 'positive' spread effect, that is, spill-over of growth from central to less favoured regions. Hirschman (1958) believed the spread effects to be stronger than the backwash effects.

A lot of effort has gone into analysing the causes of agglomeration or spatial concentration. Three causes are generally recognised: (1) economies of scale, (2) agglomeration effects, and (3) urbanisation effects. Economies of scale are inherent to the firm; agglomeration effects are the advantages to be gained by the joint location of linked productions (worked out in the attraction theory, see Klaassen, 1967), and by urbanisation effects are understood general advantages from the joint use of services etc.

In backward regions, all these advantages are largely absent; the growth-pole theory, developed in the context of regional policy, pleads their deliberate creation in regions where they are absent or insufficiently developed (Perroux, 1955; Boudeville, 1972; Paelinck, 1965; Hermansen c.s., 1970; Lasuen, 1969; etc.).

The whole body of literature referred to so far related to developments within national states. When national states form economic unions to achieve market integration, the consequences for regional development can be very important. Giersch (1949) examined the relation between agglomeration economies and regional development in an integrated market area. By his theory, if inter-European trade is freed from tariffs and quota, and factors are at liberty to move all over Europe, the result will be international, intra-European agglomeration, for integration will make a highly industrialised centre attractive to even more labour and capital. By contrast, peripheral regions will be put at a greater disadvantage than before; the peripheral regions of a country that itself is peripheral to the centre of the European Community, will suffer the most, for they will become even more peripheral in respect to the new super centre. On the other hand, regions on inner frontiers may derive some benefit from the integration.

The same problems appear a fortiori in a monetary union. As a matter of fact·Giersch (1949) already argued that "The creation of a monetary union transforms balance-of-payment problems into regional problems" ! If the participating countries vary widely in their initial stages of development, the effect of monetary integration is likely to be negative (Marquand, 1973, Stahl, 1974; Williamson, 1976).

On the other hand, integration may work positively for the regional equilibrium of an area like that of the European Community, if the growth effect it engenders for all regions surpasses any negative influence on specific regions. (The theoretical effects of integration on different types of regions is described in more detail in Vanhove and Klaassen, 1980.)

The spread of productive activities across Europe plays an important part, and location factors therefore carry great weight in location theory. We shall not continue our discussion of location theory here, but rather refer to the extensive treatise of both regional-development theory and location theory on the European level by Vanhove and Klaassen (1981).

Production factors are to some extent mobile in Europe, which is apparent from industrial movement. A fairly complete analysis (see Molle and Klaassen, 1982) in Europe has proved this movement to have often gone toward more equality (spread effects). Migration, on the contrary, has often had backwash effects (Van Haselen and Molle, 1981). The highly mobile production factor capital also tends to contribute to greater concentration.

One of the mechanisms behind that tendency works through the banks, which centralise the savings of "poor", often "peripheral", regions and use them to provide "concentration" regions with capital, because there the projects with the best financial prospects are to be found. Prospects are better in concentration regions because they are nearer to the market, are able to employ specialised manpower, etc.

Apart from the market mechanism, there are also impulses from the political system that do not always favour backward regions. Think, for instance, of the effects of the tendency towards national wage-setting, which has done away with the relative wage-cost advantage many regions used to have.

The instances given of the dynamics of regional development, to which many others could be added, may suffice to illustrate the general nature of the regional problem.

3. Regional policy: why, how, and what ?

Why do governments try to improve regional equilibria ? There are three reasons for regional policy. First, the system itself possesses no, or insufficient, self-regulating mechanisms. Second, large groups of the population experience inequality as socially inacceptable and morally unfair; this is known in the literature as the "equity argument" for regional policy. Third, there are also typically economic arguments for a regional policy, known in the literature as the so-called "efficiency argument", the consideration being that as a result of the deficient regional distribution of some production factors, government goods, and economic activity, the economy cannot fully profit from the potential available, so that total production is less than it could be if the inequalities were removed.

All countries of Western Europe have taken up regional policy in the course of the past decades. Dependent on the gravity of their regional problems and the prevailing socio-economic views they started sooner or later, and more or less intensively, as is apparent both from the number of instruments used and from the vigour with which they were applied. Gradually, however, some pattern has become visible in the multiplicity of ideas elaborated with respect to the tools of regional policy in the various member states of the European Community, and a degree of consensus is gradually cristallising out [1]; so, a few general characteristics can now be given.

These refer first of all to the regions to which regional policy is applied (designated areas). If at first the attention tended to focus almost universally on the so-called backward regions or regions struggling with structural adjustment, later on the insight became more and more general that the system of regions should be regarded as a whole and that each of its elements needed its own type of measure. About the instruments of regional policy, too, most people have largely the same ideas. In all member states the instruments applied can be divided into (1) instruments addressed to people and (2) instruments addressed to industries. The first group of instruments, in practically all countries far less important than the second, concerns mainly financial support to persons willing to move house. The important group of instruments applied to activities falls apart into financial benefits supposed to encourage investments in certain regions on the one hand (loans, grants, etc.) and on the other a large category of instruments facilitating location in certain regions. The latter instruments are almost invariable concerned with infrastructure (roads, ports, industrial sites, training of workers, public utilities, etc.) [2].

A few words are due, moreover, about the objectives at which regional policy is aimed. Some time ago the OECD summed up the objectives which the various countries of Western Europe seek to realise through their regional policy (OECD 1970); as they have remained practically unchanged since, we shall briefly represent them here. They are:

- "planning economic development and investment in accordance not only with the need to promote the overall progress of the national economy, but also with the diverse needs and potentialities of the different regions and with the geographical distribution of the population and manpower;
- reducing the imbalance between regions in the distribution of ecnomic activity and in the levels of income, prosperity and welfare;
- maintaining and encouraging the social and cultural basis of the life of the regional populations including the preservation and best use of natural, cultural and amenity resources;
- planning the physical environment and infrastructure including housing, communication,and other forms of fixed capital in

accordance with consistent and coherent national, inter-regional and regional aims and with the economic resources available."

Many authors have already posed the question of the effectiveness of regional policy: how far has it effectively contributed to the realisation of the objectives ? To answer that question, several types of studies have been carried out. The first type simply adds up all employment in activities that have received support, and considers the outcome the effect of regional policy. The question is, however, how much of this employment would also have come into being without support. To measure that, models have been developed which try to isolate the effects of regional policy from the "normal" development [3]. From such studies, regional policy generally emerges as of limited importance. Finally, studies based on interviews have been carried out, firms located somewhere being asked how far measures of regional aid had influenced their location decision. From these studies, too, the general conclusion is that no high hopes should be nursed as to the possibility of influencing the spatial distribution of economic activities by the current regional-policy measures.

4. Regional problems in de European Community

The European Community struggles with vast regional problems. The nature of these regional problems varies widely and gives rise to different types of problem regions. On the one hand there are regions that so far have hardly if at all participated in the development of industry and services and are still largely oriented to agriculture. Especially in the regions of the southern member states agriculture is often not very productive; examples are Calabria and Molise (in Italy). On the other hand there are regions which at a certain stage of economic development used to play a leading role, but which have now landed in difficulties owing to changed production conditions; clear instances are the traditional steel regions like Wallonia, Saarland, South Wales. The former group of regions is generally characterised by a peripheral situation and a deficient infrastructure, also as far as business services are concerned. The latter type of region is generally marked by inadequate infrastructure and serious problems both in old industrial and in residential areas. The labour-market situation, too, is different in the two types of regions. While in the agricultural type of region the problems are lack of schooling and lack of industrial and service traditions, the trouble with the old industrial regions is that their mostly highly specialised manpower cannot satisfy modern requirements.

Until a short time ago the so-called congestion areas were counted among the problem regions too; in contrast to the two other types, their fast growth and high concentration wanted checking. Lately, however, policy makers have become aware that these regions, mostly the central urban regions of each country, have lost their strong position and are now also struggling to adjust their economic as well as their social structure to the new conditions. They may indeed become the great problem regions of the future [4].

Among the disparities existing among the regions of Europe, the disparity in income by head is generally felt as one of the most painful. The inequality among regions in Europe on that score is rather great. The region with the highest per capita income in the European Community of Nine is five times "richer" than the poorest. The differences are represented on map 1.

The use on the European level of Gross Regional Product (GRP) by head of the population as an indicator of wealth is subject to certain errors. GRP does not indicate, for instance, the differences on the spending side (that is to say it does not account for transfer incomes). Moreover it is based on rates of exchange, which, as is well known, inadequately reflects the differences in purchasing power among countries. Finally, the figure is subject to all the well known criticisms of national product or national income as an indicator of prosperity. For lack of any beter indicator, its use is fairly general, however.

The analysis of the development of the differences in regional income by head in Europe was until recently very deficient for lack of comparable figures. Since 1970 such figures have been drawn up by Eurostat. For the purpose of an earlier publication (Molle c.s., 1980)+ we had drawn up as well, with the help of all available data, comparable figures of regional income in 76 regions in the European Community of Nine for the years 1950 and 19. These figures were used to check, among others with the help of Theil's index, how the diparity in income by head had developed between 1950 and 1970. We found it had continuously

Map 1. Gross Domestic Product by head in re gions of the EC (index EC average = 100), 1973.

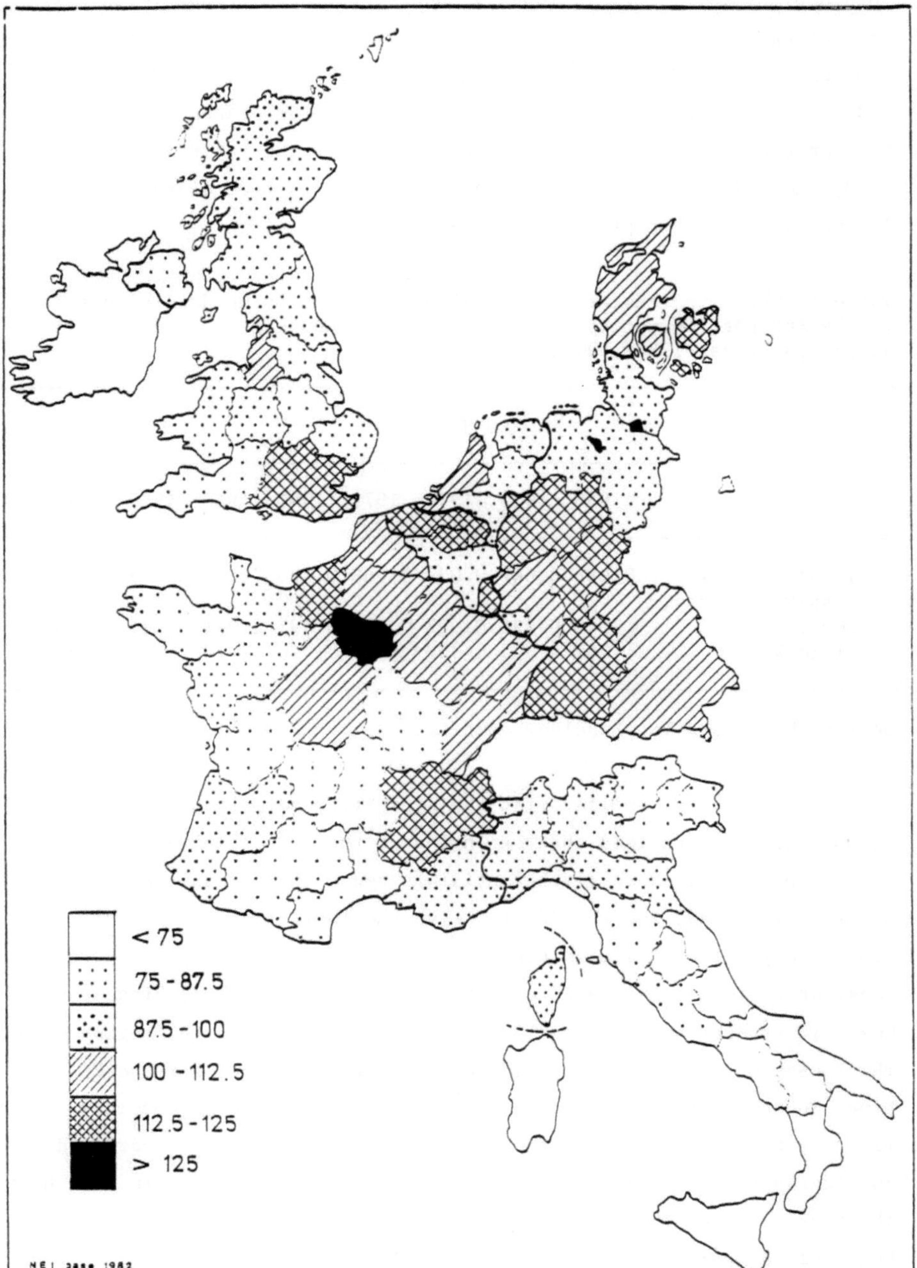

decreased. However, the period 1950-1970 is already relatively far behind us; moreover the European Community has in the meantime been joined by Greece and will probably soon be further extended with Spain and Portugal. So there was reason to carry out the analyses anew for the new Community of Twelve and a recent year(1977) (Molle and Van Haselen, 1980). The existing data base for the nine member states was completed to that end for the three new member states for the years 1950, 1960, 1970, and 1977. The results of the new computations of disparity in income by head are represented in table 1.

Table 1. Theil-indices of Gross Regional Product by head of population in the European Community (total disparity among regions and disparity among countries, 1950/1977).

	EC 9				EC 12			
	1950	1960	1970	1977	1950	1960	1970	1977
1. Total disparity	0.068	0.047	0.039	0.068	0.125	0.102	0.073	0.100
2. Disparity among countries	0.040	0.026	0.023	0.052	0.095	0.081	0.061	0.083
2 : 1 in %	59	55	59	76	76	79	78	83

Source: Molle and Van Haselen, op.cit.

No one slightly familiar with the prosperity relations existing in Europe will be surprised that extension of the EC to twelve member states appears to cause a substantial increase in regional-income disparity. Indeed, for the EC of Twelve the Theil-index was in all sample years about twice as high as for the EC of Nine. Or, in more imaginative terms: in the EC of Twelve the region with the highest Gross Domestic Product by head was 10 to 14 times richer than the region with the lowest GDP/head, as compared to 5 to 6 times richer for the EC of Nine. Though always higher than that of the EC of Nine in absolute figures, total disparity in the extended EC appeared to have dropped considerably as well in the course of the period 1950-1970, in fact by about half. After 1970 a reversed tendency is observable, however; since that year disparity has increased considerably.

Let us consider somewhat more closely the causes of this disparity and its development. That is possible by splitting the Theil-index into the disparity "between sets" and that "within sets", a set consisting of regions belonging to the same country. In table 1 (row 2) the disparity among the levels of income by head in the member states is represented and (row 3) expressed in percentages of total disparity among regions. The differences among countries appear largely determinant of the differences among regions: in the EC of Nine between 1950 and 1970 for 55 to 60 per cent, in the EC of Twelve in the same years even 75 to 85 per cent. The recent increase in total disparity appear to result entirely from the income disparity among countries; hence, even 83 per cent of the regional income-inequality indicator in the EC of Twelve in 1977 can be attributed to differences between national-income levels. Taking income by head of employed person instead of head of population pushes up this last figure to 90 per cent (Molle and Van Haselen, 1980).

So far, we have discussed only indicators of total disparity, leaving aside the position of the various regions. However, in our earlier publications we have also analysed the ranking of the European regions by several indicators, and found a remarkable stability. Throughout the analysis period of almost thirty years the peripheral regions of the Mediterranean countries were always in the lowest positions, while some urban, formerly "congested", regions in Northern Europe were steadily at the top. Only two significant shifts occurred: Germany moving strongly upward with all its regions, and the United Kingdom falling back with all its regions. Lately, though, the latter country has shown a slight upward tendency again.

Another indicator of regional disparity strongly emphasised in most discussions, is unemployment. Again, there are hardly any comparable data from official sources for the years before 1975. From the analysis of as many as possible national figures made comparable, relative unemployment in 1950 appears to have been much higher in Western Germany than elsewhere in Europe, whereas in the United Kingdom the proportion of unemployed was below the EC average. That situation has gradually changed and recently it is primarily the Italian and British regions (and Ireland) which, within the EC of Nine, have suffered from high unemployment percentages (see map 2). The figures for the three new member states are greatly deficient, but as far as they can be made comparable they appear to indicate very high unemployment. This

Map 2. Regional differences in unemployment (unemployed as a percentage of total employment), 1980 (index; EC average = 100).

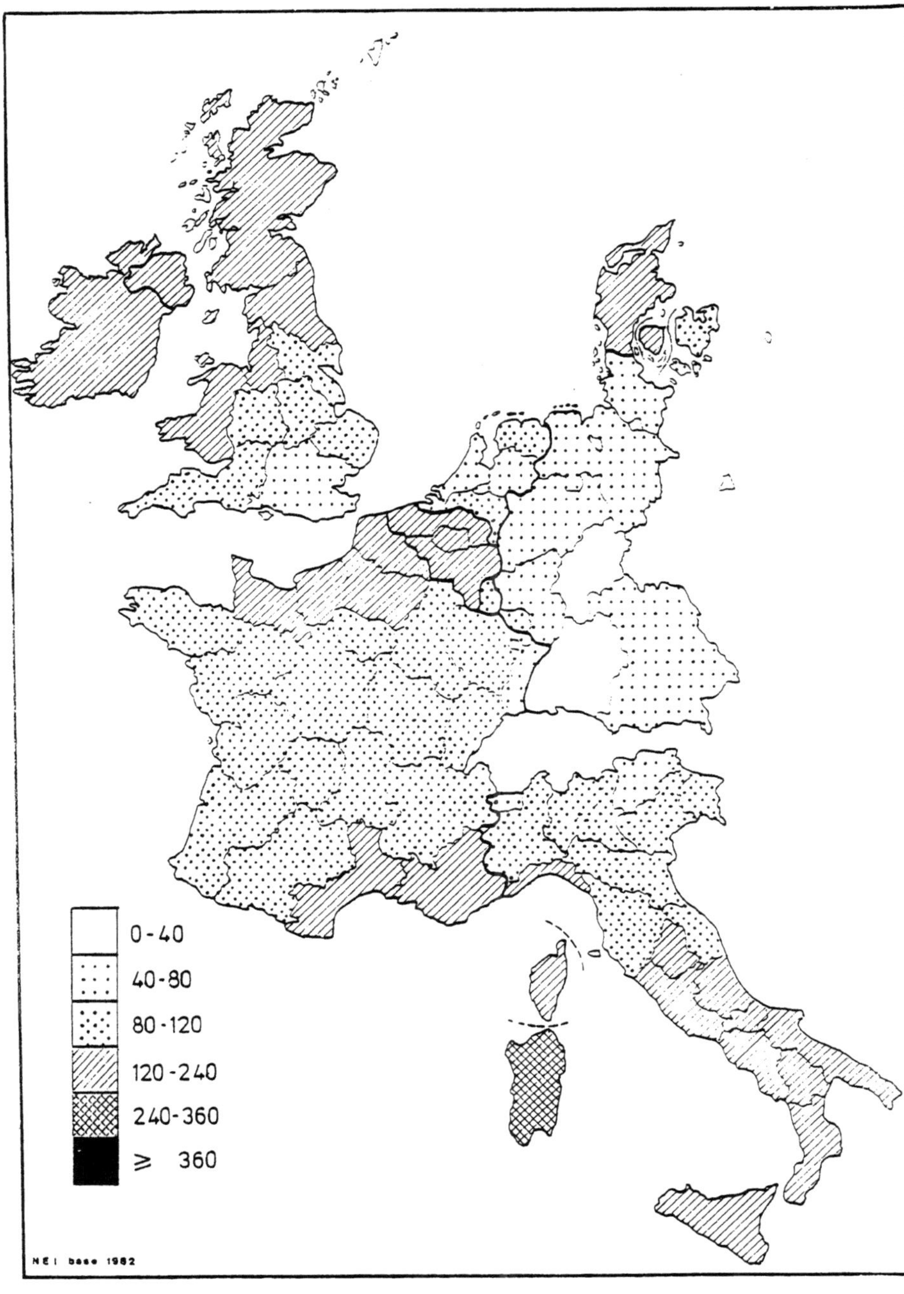

indicator again points to the strong influence of the national factor on the regional unemployment situation in Europe.

In the recent past the regional differences in income in Europe have increased, mostly because the member states themselves were showing greater disparities. A further increase of disparity must be reckoned with in the future, given the expected differences in economic growth among the twelve member states of the EC.

Why is it that Mediterranean countries are in such a bad way as to income by head and unemployment as compared to Northern Europe, and why have the relative positions of the United Kingdom and Germany changed ? Actually, all manner of national developments and situations appear responsible for the one as well as the other. The underlying factors such as the presence of resources, the level of schooling of the active population, the access to markets and in particular social and economic infrastructure, are more typically national than regional. Therefore, for the treatment of regional problems within the EC it is not sufficient to consider merely regional factors, as one would for regions within one single country; indeed, the so-called national factors should be given at least the same amount of attention.

The regional problem of Europe cannot be captured solely in terms of income by head and unemployment; however, given the weight these indicators carry in political discussions, the results of the present analysis may, with proper reserve, be used for a preliminary confrontation of regional problems with regional policy in the European Community.

5. Regional policy on the European level

Having thus briefly discussed the nature of the European regional problems we now turn to European regional policy [5]. The first question that arises is how European policy is distinct from national policy. A first difference lies in the executive agency. In the member states the policy maker is always the central government, the most complete incorporation of government authority and the umpire deciding about the equilibrium among the parts of its territory. These states themselves are regions of a larger territory, however. In the previous section we have seen that within that larger territory there are problems at least as serious as those within member states. The question then arises who is responsible for the equilibrium among these "macro" regions. Until recently the answer to that question was univocally: the states themselves. In an effort to keep their prosperity at least at par with that of other countries, they availed themselves of all possible kinds of instruments, such as monetary policy, trade policy, national growth policy, policies with respect to capital and knowledge, and sometimes even military intervention. Indeed some of these instruments were sometimes applied not only to maintain the balance among states, but also to promote the equilibrium among regions of one state; a case in point is the use of tariffs to support the textile industry, which is strongly regionally concentrated.

As Europe became united, and notably with the venue of the EC, the picture has changed somewhat. The creation of the Common Market and the development of a collective foreign-trade policy have deprived member states of some instruments they used to employ to further their national as well as regional growth. The harmonisation achieved especially on the monetary and social planes but also in some other respects has cost instruments in those fields much of their significance. Should the Economic and Monetary Union be accomplished (which for the time being is improbable), then the instruments available to national states would be curtailed even more; in that case they could no longer pursue a national policy of exchange rates. Measures of regional policy have indeed been necessary to cope with possible effects of the initial and progressive integration.

Political concern with regional equilibrium has not ended with the first stage of the Common Market and some further major steps of integration. On the contrary, the actual day-to-day function of the European Community needs to be attended constantly by adequate measures of regional policy. Structural changes due to economic, technological, environmental and social developments continue to occur, demanding progressive adaptation. The system is not self-correcting, and it seems necessary for the EC to accept responsibility for regional policy. Indeed, the functioning of the Community seems to come into jeopardy unless regional effects are corrected by a proper regional policy. A clear example gives the steel industry. The lack of alternative activities in "steel regions" has induced certain member states to give heavy support to the established industry, to which other member states have responded by a threat of closing the frontiers. Now that would mean a direct violation of the foundations of the Community (the free market), jeopardising the whole European structure, on which the prosperity of Europe has meanwhile largely come to depend.

Obviously then, there is more than enough reason, not only on the national, but also on the European level, to put forward the "economic-efficiency" argument in favour of regional policy. But the equity argument also has a European dimension, insofar as it does justice to solidarity between prosperous and less prosperous regions in Europe. The recent tendency of the European Community to emphasise social and human aspects as well as purely economic ones, also seems to point towards efforts on the European level to improve regional equilibrium by pursuing a regional policy.

The objective of European regional policy has been formulated at many places in different ways. One of the most recent official statements (EC, 1975) distinguishes two objects:

- diminishing current regional problems as they occur both in the traditionally less developed regions and in regions involved in a process of industrial or agrarian transformation;
- preventing new regional disparities that could result from structural changes in world economy, etc.

The obvious question is now what the EC does to attain these objects. At first that was only very little, especially because the EC was very badly equipped to realise such objectives. One cause was that in 1958 nobody really had an idea of the size and nature of regional problems on the European level. The Community began to function without having received sufficient authority on those scores from the Rome Treaty [6]. Getting the necessary authority turned out to be a long procedure. However, by dint of constant diligence the Commission has gradually acquired more and more instruments, and the regional element has become more and more prominent among the policy areas of the EC.

The regional policy of the European Community is conducted in co-operation with the member states. Indeed, the Community's regional policy is not a substitute for, but a complement to the regional policies carried out by the member countries.

Four main elements can usefully be distinguished.

1. An activity taken on by the Commission at an early stage was that of acquiring knowledge of the regional situation in the Community and the developments that occur in that situation. In that connection the Commission has carried out or commissioned several studies (EC 1961, 1964, 1969, 1971, 1973). The main purpose of these reports is to keep knowledge of the old problems up-to-date and to recognise new problems as soon as they present themselves. These reports also serve as a foundation for discussions with the member states about priorities to be set in regional policy and changes which may have to be carried through in this policy. In the existing studies the development of some general indicators has been given primary attention, but the intention is to study in the future the effectiveness of the policy more systematically.
2. A second task which the Commission had given itself was to co-ordinate its own policy in a number of policy areas, such as those of agriculture, social affairs, coal and steel, energy, economy, transport, foreign trade. Many policy measures taken in these fields influence regional development. Knowledge of their respective influence in the context of total policy should make it possible to formulate policy under consideration of the regional element. That aspect is very important, financially first of all, given the sums granted by the Social Fund and the Agricultural Fund and those provided by the European Investment Bank and the European Coal and Steel Community as loans. A recent report has shown, for instance, that the EC's agriculture expenditure are favouring rich North-European regions more than poor, South-European ones (Henry, 1981).
3. A third task of the Commission in the setting of regional policy is the co-ordination of activities of member states. As early as 1965 this was recognised as necessary, and a proposal was submitted to draw up regional programmes for the EC's problem regions. It took almost 10 years until that proposal was accepted, but at the moment a large number of policy programmes have already been published [14]. Their purpose is, by establishing clearly what measures are being taken by the various relevant organisations in these regions

(infrastructure, schooling, housing,etc.), to enable the EC to co-ordinate these measures, identify any gaps,and developing schemes to fill up these gaps. Apart from that the reports are to serve as a base for checking the progress of regional developments. Two important points deserve to be underlined in connection with the Commission's international co-ordinating role. The first refers to an institutional provision: to let the co-ordination between the EC and the member states proceed smoothly and create a platform for regular discussions of such matters as priorities, programmes, etc., the Committee for Regional Policy was installed. This Committee consists of officials of the Commission and the national governments of the member states (the institutional structure of the EC does not provide for direct contact of Brussels with the institutions of the regions in member states). The other important provision with respect to co-ordination was of a directly regulating nature; it concerned the restriction of the support a member state may give nationally to developments in certain regions. This subsidy restriction was needed because the support to the less developed regions threatened to be completely undermined by the fact that quite large benefits could also be drawn by the more developed regions. The point is worth mentioning because here the restriction of the member states' ability to use certain instruments was actually at stake. The regulation has so far been the only one of its kind.

4. A fourth and last element that was finally given substance (in 1975) after years of negociations [8] is the possibility which the the European Community acquired with the erection of the Regional Fund of intervening directly with financial means to contribute to the development of certain regions [9]. The Fund provides credits to stimulate investments in economic activities as well as credits for the development of the infrastructure. An important condition for support to investments in activities is that these activities are already receiving aid from the member state or one of its agencies. The EC intervention is indeed meant to complement the support already given by the member states. Apart from works directly related to industrial activities (industrial sites and such), more general infrastructural works, for instance in the field of road

and canal construction, qualify for support. Member states submit projects, which are judged in the light of the "regional programme" as to their contribution to the solution of the region's problems. The Fund is fed by contributions from the various member states (the Community's own means). The financial means of the Regional Fund are distributed by a key that strongly favours low-income countries. The Fund possesses, apart from its current means, the so-called "quota section", also a so-called "non-quota section"; this relatively small section (approximately 5 per cent) can be used by the Commission to help regions in acute difficulties. In practice these funds are destined to regions suffering from negative consequences of Community policy in other fields than regional policy.

6. New regional developments; new policy proposals

Since the crisis of the early 'seventies, a number of changes have occurred in in the general economic and regional development of Europe. A first factor of change was the decrease in production growth and hence in the demand for labour. A new industrial revival is generally felt to be needed and everywhere the accent is now laid on on innovation to stimulate a thorough restructuring of the productive forces of Europe. The stagnation of the economy called a halt to two equilibrating mechanisms, namely, the migration of industry towards the less developed areas, and the migration of people towards the congested areas. Indeed, a considerable return migration has set in since 1974, seriously aggravating the unemployment problem in the traditional out-migration areas. As mentioned before, some of the traditonally strong central areas have become urban-decay areas, and industrial adaptation problems now tend to become general in Europe. However, that does not mean that disparities are vanishing; on the contrary, some regions by all development criteria continue to rank so much lower than others that there is still a clear case for regional aid to the less favoured regions.

The changes just described have grave implications for regional policy. As a matter of fact, regional policy used to rely very much on mobile industry, and the sources for that type of activity now having dried up, the development of each region now needs to be based on its own indigenous potential. Moreover, regions have to be innovative, for no standard solutions from outside can be hoped for any more. The consequences of these changes were recently evaluated by the European Commission, and proposals have been put forward to reorient EC policy(EC, 1981). These proposals emphasise the need for new instruments making for a better exploitation of the regions' indigenous development potential. Such instruments come under two headings: helping existing companies to expand, and providing the infrastructure needed to stimulate innovation. To the former category belong proposals to assist companies in obtaining advice on management and organisation questions, allowances for the development of new products, etc. To the second category belong proposals to create agencies for compiling and distributing information on product innovation and technological innovation, and for evaluating the prospects of markets and the technical feasibility of production processes. Such measures intend first and foremost to provide services to small and medium-sized companies, which otherwise would have no access to such essential information for operating efficiently [10].

We have already indicated that the development of certain regions is far below the European mean and tends to stay that way. To increase the effectiveness of regional policy, the Commission proposes to direct larger amounts from the Fund to these long-standing problem areas, in particular with a view to the enlargement of the EC. In practice that would mean that the "quota section" would be completely devoted to the regions of countries like Italy and Greece, the United Kingdom and Ireland. A new kind of "non-quota section" is proposed tot assist the regions most grievously affected by recent serious problems of industrial decline and/or by the consequences of certain Community policies (to a maximum of 20 per cent of the total Regional Fund).

Finally, the Commission proposes the elaboration of programme aid rather than project aid, and some improvements to the administration of aid measures.

The proposals of the Commission have formed the object of a long debate of the member countries and in the European Parliament. At the moment of writing this part of the book (August 1982) the outcome is not yet certain.

7. European regional policy on the right track ?

In the previous sections we have found the regional disparities in an extended European Community to be associated to a large extent with disparities among member states. We also found that the set of tools collected and still being added to in the European Community for the purpose of eliminating these disparities, is not in fact very different from those used for regional policy on the national level. Their aim is to give financial impulses to investors willing to locate in a so-called problem area, and (much more important in terms of the funds donated) to create the infrastructure required to lift problem regions out of their unfavourable position.

The limited effectiveness of these instruments on the national level has already been pointed out. There are no data available which would suggest that they are more effective on the European level. To choose instruments of regional policy for the policy within member states seems logical, but one wonders whether the simple transposal of these instruments to the European level is the most effective way of solving Europe's regional problem. Another question is whether the existing instruments are adequate in view of the volume and persistence of the regional problem on the one hand and the differences among member states on the other. In the light of current and future problems the present size of the Fund seems inadequate to realise its objective.

However, one should keep in mind that sums can be transferred from one member state to another not only through the Regional Fund but also through other EC-funds, especially the Agricultural Fund and the Social Fund. Apart from that, member states facing structural adjustment problems receive help from the European Investment Bank and the Coal and Steel Community, and financial means are also provided in the framework of the European Monetary System. The sums involved in all these schemes is a multiple of those granted by the European Regional Fund.

Besides these visible transfers there are of course also various far less tangible transfers of money, but these flows are all directly related with the total functioning of international trade and the movement of capital and are so complicated that we prefer to leave them out of the present discussion.

If the objective of greater regional equality in Europe is taken seriously, the measures described above should in practice lead to a larger flow of money from the richer to the poorer member states. The question then arises by what manner of policy such flows ought to be directed. Since the nature and volume of regional problems in the EC appears to depend on the causes of different growth rates among member states rather than on structural regional problems, the obvious thing to do is to plead a considerable increase of the financial means that can be used for a general growth and structure policy in the poorer member states rather than the intensified use of classical tools of regional policy. (One point should be emphasised however which might distort the whole picture rather seriously, namely the fact that means obtainable for purposes of regional development from the EC are used by member states to replace the sums they would otherwise have provided for that purpose themselves. Thus indirectly the "regional" means actually benefit the entire financial household of the member states.)

To recognise the desirability of providing more means does not yet imply that they are in fact provided. Evidently, a much greater appeal will have to be made to European solidarity, a notion that so far has not been brought in practice very much. On the contrary, member states, though co-operating in the Community, do so in free competition, every country trying to get the better of the others in the various negociations. The whole decision-making mechanism of the European Community would have to be changed thoroughly to make it solidarity-oriented. That in times of economic decline the richer countries will be found willing to transfer large sums of money, is hard to imagine.

However, that is not to say that nothing at all can be done to perfect the instruments of regional policy. Without financial consequence, the analyses which the Commission ought to make of the regional influence of all sorts of government measures in the EC and the member states could be reinforced. If that is done on a fairly wide scale, the discrepancy between object and means can always be pointed out; when policy measures are seen to work out clearly negatively on certain regions, a warning can be given and political forces mobilised to bring about an adjustment. Furthermore efforts can be made to destine the various funds more than in the past exclusively to the most underdeveloped regions; expansion of the total volume of these funds remains necessary, of course.

The increasing interplay of regional and national problems in the European Community may give rise to the question whether regional policy in the strict sense of the word on the level of the Community is still necessary and whether the whole regional policy could not better be left to the member states themselves. The answer to the latter question could be yes if there were mechanisms to foster the equilibrium among member states. Because that is not so in practice, the limited instruments, though perhaps not the most adequate, are still better than nothing at all. Even if such mechanisms existed however, some form of European regional policy would still be desirable to check on the European level the spatial consequences of certain measures and as far as possible compensate for them. That would be better than having the problems attacked afterwards by the member states. To the same extent that the EC wants to keep informed about the sectoral dimension of its policy (or the social, monetary, third-world dimensions, etc.) is it necessary for the spatial element to be represented in its total policy.

Notes

1. See in this connection K. Allen (1979).

2. A detailed survey of both groups of measures in force in each country now or in the past has been given in the book by Allen and others previously cited, to which we may refer.

3. For a general discussion, see B. Ashcroft (1982), C.P.A. Bartels, C.P.A., and J.J. van Duyn (1981). and in particular for some more specific techniques: H. Folmer (1980).

4. See in this connection among others L.H. Klaassen, W.T.M. Molle and J.H.P. Paelinck (eds) (1981) and L. v.d. Berg c.s. (1982).

9. For a more extensive treatment of regional policy on the European level the reader is referred to N. Vanhove and L.H. Klaassen (1980), and to a somewhat earlier publication by J. van Ginderachter (1973).

6. The best known right of the Commission of the European Community (art. 93 of the Treaty) was that of prohibiting certain measures of support, regional ones among them, if these were considered incompatible with the common market.

7. See for a survey, EC (1979).

8. Discussed already at Messina (1956), proposed formally by the Commission in 1969.

9. See for further information on the realisation of the Fund R.B.Talbot (1977).

10. Proposals for a more detailed programme for such a regional-innovation policy for the EC are contained in Molle 1982 (PRESTO study).

REFERENCES

Allen, K. c.s. (1979), "Regional Incentives in the European Community; a Comparative Study" EC collection studies, Regional Policy Series No.15, Brussels.

Andrews, R.B. (1953/1956), "Mechanics of the Urban Economic Base", series of articles in "Land Economics", Vols. 29 to 31.

Berg, L. van den, Drewett, R., Klaassen, L.H., Rossi, A. and Vijverberg, C,(1982), "Urban Europe, a Study of Growth and Decline", Pergamon Press, London.

Boudeville, J.R. (1972), "Aménagement du territoire et polarisation", Génin, Paris.

European Community (1961), "Document de la Conférence sur les économies régionales", vol. II, Brussels.

European Community (1964), "Reports by groups of experts on Regional Policy in the European Economic Community, Brussels.

European Community (1969), "A Regional Policy for the Community", Brussels.

European Community (1971), "Regional Development in the Community: Analytical Survey", Brussels.

European Community (1973), "Report on the Regional Problems in the Enlarged Community" (Thomson Report), Com.73/550, Brussels.

European Community (1979), "The Regional Development Programmes", Brussels, Regional Policy Series, nr. 17.

European Community (1981), "Proposal for a Council Regulation amending the Regulation (EEC), no. 724/75 establishing a European Regional Development Fund", Brussels.

Giersch, H. (1949), "Economic Union between Nations and the Location of Industries", Review of Economic Studies, vol. 17, pp. 87-97.

Ginderachter, J. van (1973), "La politique régionale de la Communauté, justifications, modalités et propositions", Revue du Marché Commun no.170, pp.469-486.

Hall, P. and Hay, D. (1980), "Growth Centers in the European Urban System", Heinemann, London.

Haselen, H. van, and Molle, W.T.M. (1981), "Regional Patterns of Natural Population Growth and Migration in the EC of Twelve", NEI/FEER, 1981/12, Rotterdam.

Henry, P., "Study of the Regional Impact of the Common Agricultural Policy", Luxemburg, 1981.

Hermansen, T. (c.s.) (1970), "A Review of the Concepts and Theories of Growth Poles and Growth Centers", UN Research Institute for Social Development, Geneva.

Hirschmann, A.O. (1958), "The Strategy of Economic Development", Yale University Press, New Haven, Conn.

Klaassen, L.H. (1967), "Methods of Selecting Industries for Depressed Areas", OECD, Paris.

Klaassen, L.H., Molle, W.T.M. and Paelinck J.H.P. (ed.) (1981), "Dynamics of Urban Development", Gower, Farnbourough.

Lasuên, J.R. (1969), "On Growth Poles", Urban Studies, vol. 6, pp. 137-161.

Marquand, J. (1973), "Report on Repercussions of Economic and Monetary Union on Regional Development", Cons. Assembly Council of Europe, Doc.3282, Strassburg.

Massey, D.B. (1973), "The Basic-Service Categorisation in Planning", Regional Studies, vol. 7, pp. 1-15.

Molle, W. (1980), with the collaboration of B. van Holst and H. Smit, "Regional Disparity and Economic Development in the European Community", Saxon House, Farnborough.

Molle, W.T.M. and Haselen, H. van (1980), "Regional Disparity and Assisted Areas in the European Community of Twelve", NEI/FEER, 1980/22, Rotterdam; also published in Spanish in: Revista de Estudios Regionales no.6, 1980, pp.153-197.

Molle, W.T.M. (1982), "Prospects of Regional Employment and Scanning of Technological Options", PRESTO Synthesis Report, NEI, Rotterdam.

Molle, W.T.M. and Klaassen, L.H. (ed.) (1982), "Industrial Migration and Mobility in the European Community", Gower Press, Aldershot.

Myrdal, G. (1957), "Economic Theory and Underdeveloped Regions", Duckworth, London.

OECD (1970), "The Regional Factor in Economic Development, Policies in fifteen industrialised OECD countries", OECD, Paris.

Paelinck, J.H.P. (1965), "La théorie du développement régional polarisé", Cahiers de l'ISEA (Série L, no. 15, Economies Régionales), pp.5-47.

Paelinck, J.H.P. and Nijkamp, P. (1976), "Operational Theory and Method in Regional Economics", Saxon House, Lexington (Mass.).

Perroux, F. (1955), "Note sur la notion pôle de croissance", Economie

Appliquée, vol. 8, pp. 307-320.

Pfouts, R.W. (1957), "An Empirical Testing of the Economic Base Theory", Journal of the American Institute of Planners, vol.23, no.2.

Richardson, H.W. (1973), "Regional Growth Theory", MacMillan, London.

Talbot, R.B. (1977), "The European Community's Regional Fund 1977: Progress in Planning, vol. 8, part 3, pp. 183-281.

Vanhove, N., Klaassen, L.H. (1980), "Regional Policy, a European Approach", Gower, Farnbourough.

Williamson, J. (1976), "The Implication of European Monetary Integration for the Peripheral Areas", in Vaizey, J. (ed.) "Economic Sovereignty and Regional Policy", Gill and Macmillan, Dublin.

PART FIVE

TRADE AND MONETARY POLICIES

by Peter Coffey

Trade Policies

The Theoretical Background

Writing, earlier this year, the author described the European Economic Community as being a "large customs union which is trying to establish an economic and monetary union and which finds itself in the middle of the largest free trade area in the world. The Common Market is then the world's largest and most important trading bloc."[1)]

In a few words, this description sums up the EEC and its overall trading picture. Like other customs unions, the Community has, at all times, found itself placed before three basic choices regarding trading policies. These three choices are policies of self-sufficiency (or autarchy), open-ness or the adoption of a middle road policy which lies somewhere between the first two extremes. Also, EEC trading policies have been influenced by a number of factors which have included the Common Market's basic structure, historical trading links (e.g. with former colonies), internal economic policies and the pressures of certain lobbies - particularly the agricultural and textile ones.

Starting with the birth of the EEC, the author has deduced seven principles on which the Community's trading policies have been based. These principles are:

1. The EEC (with the exception of the United Kingdom and its supplies of North Sea oil and coal reserves in that and some other countries) is not self-sufficient in supplies of energy and raw materials. Therefore, these commodities have generally been allowed to enter the Community either free of duty or with very low tariffs.

2. At the end of the transitional period, the Common External Tariff (CET) would consist of the average of the existing

Coffey, P. (ed.): Main Economic Policy Areas of the EEC
©1983. Martinus Nijhoff Publishers, The Hague / Boston / London
ISBN 90-247-2793-6.

(1957) tariffs of the Member States. Subsequent participation by the EEC in a series of international trade negotiations have resulted in a rather low average CET.

3. It was agreed that special arrangements would be made for existing overseas territories, dependencies and the like for which Member States exercised responsibility. This policy has evolved over time from the special arrangements made for such countries to the two Yaoundé Agreements and further on to the present Second Lomé Agreement.

4. At the outset, the Community decided to embark upon the construction of a Common Agricultural Policy (CAP) and until the Common Agricultural Market (CAM) actually came into being the EEC was unwilling to discuss the question of agricultural matters in international trade negotiations. Since the full achievement of the CAM, its existence has tended to negatively influence the Community's trade relations with most parts of the world - especially with Eastern Europe, Australasia and Latin America.

5. The Community expressed its willingness to enter into international trade negotiations with non-Community countries. Subsequently, the EEC has been (together with the USA and more recently - Japan) the principal protagonist in such negotiations. As a result as mentioned in point 2, and following the Tokyo Round Negotiations, the average CET is now rather low.

6. Partly as a consequence of the low CET and partly due to the increased competitive ability of a growing number of Third World countries (particularly in the fields of clothing and textiles) the EEC has, since the 1970's increasingly resorted to non-tariff barriers of a "voluntarist" nature which are sometimes described as Orderly Marketing Arrangements (OMA's) or Voluntary Export Restrictions (VER's). Currently, efforts are being made to "persuade" Japan to restrict exports of cars and electronic products to EEC Member States.

7. Since the mid 1970's, the Community has started to move in the direction of attempting to secure its supplies of

energy and raw materials.[2] This more recent policy is an obvious reaction to the lack of self-sufficiency in these fields - which was mentioned in point 1.

Although these basic principles do clearly explain the Community's trading attitudes and policies towards imports and exports of agricultural products, raw materials, energy and some 'sensitive' products, they do not necessarily explain the choice or lack of choice of policies for specific geographical areas - about which so much has been written. Therefore, it is useful to examine such areas for which policies have or have not been made.

The Community's Trading Policies

The number of geographical areas for which specific policies have been evolved is, in reality, rather small. There exist policies for a group of Third World countries, for Eastern Europe, for the Mediterranean and for EFTA countries. There is, however, no specific policy for the Community's most important individual trading partner - the United States. Instead, the Common Market tends to meet or confront the Americans in international trade, monetary and energy negotiations. Similarly, no specific policy has been defined for Japan.

The one geographical area for which a consistent and continuous trade policy has existed is for a group of Third World countries - more specifically - for Africa. Already at the Venice meeting in 1956, France had threatened not to join the Common Market if special arrangements were not made for her African colonies and dependencies. Such arrangements were subsequently made, and, as these countries became independent, a more formal arrangement (of which there were two), the Yaoundé Agreement, was made.[3] With the impending British membership of the EEC, arrangements obviously had to be made for a number of Commonwealth countries. These arrangements, the Lomé Agreements, which were made with the ACP States (African, Caribbean and Pacific States) have raised great expectations among Third World countries. These expectations are analysed in the next part of this study.

Apart from individual agreements made with individual Third World countries, it was felt that more formal international arrangements should be made to cover products of interest and importance to a large number of Third World countries not participating earlier in the Yaoundé and more recently in the Lomé Agreements. The resulting arrangement was the Generalised System of Preferences (G.S.P.'s) which is a 'generalised, non-reciprocal system of preferences' and is organised on the basis of duty-free quotas. The EEC introduced this scheme in 1971 and renewed it annually for a period of ten years. In 1981, it was renewed for a further decade. However, the quotas have now been adjusted so as to penalise the efficient Third World producers. This situation is further examined in the next part of this study.

At first sight, it may seem strange that one is able to observe attempts by the EEC to adopt a common policy towards Eastern Europe since 1960. Whilst fairly obvious reasons seemed to exist for the creation of policies for Africa and the Mediterranean, such reasons did not seem to exist for the adoption of a common policy towards Eastern Europe. Nevertheless, there were two fundamental and important reasons which made the Community feel it necessary to adopt a common attitude towards these countries. First, the EEC feared the dumping of products at very low prices in any one or a group of EEC Member States by East European countries. Second, the Soviet Union did not recognise the EEC as a legal entity - therefore, the Community felt it necessary to find some means of persuading the Russians to accept its legal existence. The weapon used in both these situations has been the "Community Clause" which the Council agreed in 1960, should be place in all trade agreements. In reality, this weapon has only been properly used since 1973.

Under the influence of its agricultural policy, the EEC also formulated and accepted a resolution which could be used against CMEA or any other countries whose exports of agricultural products might threaten its CAP and CAM. This regulation

(No.3/63) enables the Commission to stop certain agricultural imports if it considered, after consultations with a Committee of experts from Member States, that the objectives of the CAP might be threatened.

The policy for the Mediterranean has been much less clear and more complex than that for Eastern Europe. Individual bilateral arrangements between the Community and Mediterranean countries have been made since the early 1960's. However, it is only since 1972/3 that one has been able to talk of a coherent policy - the creation, by the Common Market, of a Mediterranean Free Trade Area. Since that date attempts have been made by the Community to co-ordinate the agreements with Mediterranean - and particularly with North African countries.

This apparent co-ordination of the Community's Mediterranean Policy now appears to be in the process of being jeopardised by the planned Second Enlargement. Already, (as from January 1981) Greece is an EEC Member State, and negotiations are in progress for the admission of Portugal and Spain. The possible membership of these two countries would have the most disastrous and profound consequences for the relations of the Common Market with Mediterranean and other countries. These possible consequences are examined in the next part of this study.

A policy for the EFTA countries only began with Britain's membership of the Common Market. Indeed, the United Kingdom had made her own entry into the EEC conditional upon the making of arrangements for other EFTA countries. Thus, using the same five year transitional period for the alignment of tariffs as that given to the British, the EFTA countries were offered preferential trade agreements with the rather rigid rules of origin as used under the Yaoundé Agreements. As was to be expected, during the transitional period, the existing trade deficits of the EFTA countries with the EEC increased and there was a substantial degree of trade integration by the EFTA countries with the Community. Also, there is evidence of trade diversion from Third World and other countries (formerly important trading partners of the EFTA countries) in favour of the Common Market.

As has already been stressed, the geographical areas for which the clearest policies have been laid down, i.e., the ACP States and Eastern Europe, are not (see: table 1), in terms of value, particularly important trading partners for the Community. In comparison, both the Mediterranean and the EFTA countries are more important partners, whilst the United States, for which country no specific arrangement exists, is the most important single trading partner of the Common Market. There exist (as there have always existed) nevertheless, important areas of contention between the Common Market and the United States. There also exists a growing agreement area about protectionism between the two sides against imports of textiles and clothing from efficient Third World countries and against imports of cars and electrical goods from Japan. Thus, it appears that the two most important economic and trading blocs in the Western World are becoming increasingly tempted to adopt protectionist policies.

The Community's Trading Options for the 1980's

Two of the basic seven principles, listed by the author at the beginning of this part of the study, are almost certainly likely to be the rock on which the EEC will build its trading policies in the 1980's. The Community (with a few notable exceptions) being still not self-sufficient in supplies of raw materials and energy, will be forced to import such commodities at zero or low tariff ratings and to seek to enhance the security of such supplies. This latter point is underlined by the signing of long-term agreements by a number of Common Market countries (notably West Germany) with the Soviet Union for supplies of natural gas. Similarly, the Community agreed in 1982, to borrow 600 million U.S. dollars in the international money market to lend to the Brazilian state enterprise Copanhia Vale do Rio Doce to exploit the massive deposits of iron ore at Carajas in the Eastern part of the Amazon.

The other quasi eternal pillar of and influence on all the Community's internal and external economic policy is agriculture - or more precisely - the CAP. This policy has at all times - and will continue to negatively - influence(d) the EEC's relations with all countries. Doubtlessly, mainly for political reasons, a few little concessions will be given here and there, but, the problem will remain. Furthermore, this whole question will be complicated in a much more dramatic fashion by the possible Second Community Enlargement. Already, the EEC is nearly self-sufficient (as explained below) and even has a surplus in the production of a number of Mediterranean agricultural products. With the possible membership of Portugal and Spain, the situation is likely to become dramatic. To mention only one example, what is going to happen to Tunesia which exports about 80 per cent of its total output of oil to the EEC?

Apart from temperate agricultural products which the Community classifies as being 'sensitive' products, in the non-agricultural field, the case of textiles and clothing is about as serious, according to present evidence, in this specific area, the EEC is most likely to persist in its policy of protectionism in the 1980's.

The evidence for this forecast is threefold. Firstly, in the 1970's and the early 1980's the Community has persistently invited a number of countries in all parts of the world to restrict their exports of textiles and clothing to the Common Market on a 'voluntary' basis. Even a possible future Member State, Portugal, has been informed that it should control its exports of textiles to the rest of the Community during the transitional phase!

Secondly, the EEC, in the further renewal of the Multi-Fibre Agreement at the end of 1981, only agreed to do so if, subsequently (implying during the course of 1982), the Third World signatories accepted the Community's rigid ceilings on imports of these products, which would be negotiated on an individual country - by country basis.

Thirdly, in its agreement to renew the G.S.P.'s for a further decade as from 1981, the EEC re-aligned the quotas so as to penalise the efficient Third World countries. It is questionable as to whether the poorer countries for which quotas have been increased will be able to fulfill them.

Failing some unexpected revolutionary change in attitudes, the author fears that the Community's protectionist stance vis-à-vis imports of textiles and clothing from Third World countries will deepen now that the United States is moving towards the Common Market in this field. Within the EEC itself, in a country such as West Germany, formerly noted for its open and free trade attitudes, the protectionist lobby is making considerable progress. This development is likely to strengthen the attitudes of the French and British which tend to be strongly protectionist.

Do all these observations imply that the Community has resolutely opted for the option of protectionism for the 1980's? The answer, at this moment in time (1982), can only be a mixed one. Further, it is wise to balance the adoption of an attitude or policy on the one hand - and the possible implementation thereof on the other. In the case of the two areas of products under examination - agriculture and textiles and clothing - the Community (other things remaining equal) does appear to have adopted a resolutely protectionist stance and to, at least temporarily, have rejected a policy of "product differentiation".[4)]

To the author, the important option of "product differentiation" - essential for the survival of such a technologically advanced groups of countries such as the EEC - has never really been examined clearly. It is just possible - even in the field of agriculture - that the Second Enlargement may as a matter of necessity encourage the Community to choose precisely this option. The author would submit that, during the course of the 1980's, a number of challenges may persuade the Common Market to adopt a more constructive option between now and the end of the decade.

Challenges to the European Economic Community

With possible one exception (international commodity agreements), the challenges to the Common Market during the

1980's are likely to come from geographical areas and/or groupings and from individual countries. Thus, the author would list the following areas and countries as presenting a challenge to the EEC. The nature of the challenge will be examined and proposals made regarding the possible options which might be adopted. Challenges will most probably be presented by the Second Community Enlargement and the Mediterranean, Eastern Europe, the United States, Japan, China, and the Asean States.

The Third World

The model for co-operation between the West and the Third World is, and, in the foreseeable future, is likely to be the Lomé Agreements - and - just possibly the G.S.P.'s.

The Lomé Agreements have been especially notable for three things, the Stabex Arrangements, the commodity agreements for EEC imports of rum, bananas, and sugur from the ACP countries and for the principle of non-reciprocity as enshrined in the Agreements. A potentially important factor in Lomé II is the adoption of new rules of origin (similarly to those formerly used by EFTA) which allow the ACP countries to use a "cumulation of origin" principle - thus encouraging more economic integration between these states.

Until nearly the end of Lomé I, the Stabex Arrangements seemed to function surprisingly well. However, in 1980, as a result of unusually depressed prices for coffee and groundnuts, the Scheme came under acute financial pressure and it was found necessary to draw on 20 per cent of the funds allocated for 1981. Also, in 1980, only between 57 and 58 per cent of the requests for financial assistance were granted. This unsatisfactory situation has continued through 1981 and into 1982. Most recently, the problem has been cocoa and it seems that the financial requirements for supporting this commodity are quite insatiable. It is also unlikely, if not impossible, that the Community itself could solve the problem of this commodity. Although an International Cocoa Agreement has come on stream, the world's most important consumer, the

United States and one of the most important producers, Ivory Coast, are not signatories to this Agreement.

In the short run, unless the EEC is willing to place larger financial resources at the disposal of the Stabex Scheme - which is unlikely - the Scheme is likely to be reduced in scope and to cause profound disappointment to the ACP States. In the long run, the solution may be found in the participation of the EEC and the United States in the United Nations Common Fund - linked to existing commodity schemes. This Fund is unlikely, however, to come on stream before 1984.

Whilst awaiting the possible enlargement of the Stabex Scheme into a much larger international scheme, the list of products covered deserve greater examination. To date, only basic commodities have been covered. This, unfortunately, seems to condemn the Third World signatories to remain at a primary stage of economic activity. One means of changing this situation would be to include in the list of products which have gone some degree of transformation.

The Generalised System of Preferences (G.S.P.'s), being a non-reciprocal duty-free quota system of preferences for manufactures and semi-manufactures is one of the best schemes that has ever been thought up for encouraging the economic and industrial development of Third World countries. Unfortunately, during the course of its first decade of life (1971 - 1980) certain criticisms were levied against the operation of the system concerning an undue complexity of management and the use, by the EEC, of lists of 'sensitive' and 'semi-sensitive' products. The scheme was, nevertheless, improved during that time period. However, in renewing the G.S.P.'s for a further decade as from 1981, the Community has decided to reduce the quotas which may be used by the most developed Third World countries such as South Korea. In fact, these countries are being penalised for being efficient! Similarly, with the renewal of the Multi-Fibre Agreement (MFA) at the end of 1981 and early 1982 the EEC has been generally regressive in its offers of restricted quotas on a 'take it or leave it basis'.

All these moves bode ill for future relations between the

Community and Third World Countries and the situation may only be solved by the active adoption by the EEC of policies of "product differentiation" and participation in the Common Fund and international commodity schemes. However, even if these policies were adopted, all the Community's trading partners will be faced by the problems associated with the second enlargement.

The Second Enlargement - Possible Consequences for the Community's Mediterranean Policy and other Trade Relations

In reality, the accession of Greece, Spain and Portugal will have a mixture of consequences for the Community and for non-EEC countries. At the outset, it should be said that the three new Member States display the following characteristics:

(i) They are not self-sufficient in supplies of temperate foodstuffs, notably: maize, meat, sugar cereals and butter.

(ii) They grow large amounts of Mediterranean agricultural products and have surpluses - notably of wines, olive oil, tomatoes and citrus fruits.

(iii) With the exception of Spain, these three countries are not major industrial powers. However, they do possess a comparative advantage in the fields of clothing and textiles, and, in some cases, for steel and ship-building. These, of course, are considered by the present Common Market to be 'sensitive' products.

Should present EEC rules and policies remain unchanged, then, the following possible results may take place when Portugal and Spain, like Greece - which is already a member, enter the EEC. There will be increased surpluses in Community supplies of Mediterranean agricultural products (notably: wines, olive oil and citrus fruits) and in 'sensitive' industrial products. This implies that the possibilities of maintaining the present trade levels with other Mediterranean countries will be reduced.

There is, however, likely to be a considerable benefit for the Northern farmers in the present Community. The new Member States will be encouraged to make good their shortfall of supplies of temperate foods from EEC sources rather than from their traditional non-Community suppliers. This will have negative effects on the EEC's relations with North and South America and other parts of the world. Thus, what should the Community do?

It is almost certain that if the Common Market does not change its present policies, then non-EEC countries whose trade with the Community will be damaged by the accession of the three new Member States will demand compensation - as is their right according to the GATT. In this context, it should be noted that this was the reaction of the United States following the First Community Enlargement. Already apparently, the Commission is studying the possibility of the granting of compensation to trade partners who will suffer injury.

The other possible alternative is to change Community policies. Immediately, the CAP is an obvious candidate for such reform. At least, in this area - as well as in some industrial sectors, a policy encouraging quality (especially for wines) rather than quantity should be adopted as a matter of urgent necessity.

The author considers that the Community's diplomatic and trade relations with North and South America and with other parts of the world are too important to be jeopardised by non-preparation in advance of the Second Enlargement. Further the danger exists that should the EEC not change some of its basic policies, then countries outside the Common Market will retaliate, perhaps by cutting down imports from the EEC or placing high tariffs on such goods. Both Australia and the United States have, in the past, made such threats. Similarly, some countries may decide not to place important contracts with Community countries for capital investment projects. A precedent for such a possibility may be found in the action of Indonesia, in 1981, when that country threatened not to go ahead with the placing of an important capital investment project with the United Kingdom in retaliation for the placing of British curbs on imports of Indonesian clothing.

Other Areas of Possible Contention

As has just been stressed, the Second Enlargement will most probably cause a deterioration in relations between the EEC with most non-Community countries. However, with some states or groups of countries there always exist contentious issues and it is unlikely that these will be solved to any appreciable degree in the 1980's. Among the most actual of issues are trade relations with the United States and with Eastern Europe.

The United States

The European Economic Community is in the process (1982) of embarking upon a major trade war with the United States. The product at the centre of this war is steel and the American accusation that Common Market (and other) countries are subsidising the production of steel. Already, at the end of 1981 and during the first half of 1982, contacts aimed at reaching a compromise took place between the two sides. Unfortunately, with the preliminary decision, announced on 11 June 1982, by the U.S. Commerce Department, to impose countervailing duties on 21 European, Brazilian and South African countries (accused by the Americans of subsidising steel production in violation of GATT rules) a trade war between the two sides seems inevitable.

The fundamental problem between the United States and the Community is that they, together with Japan, are the main protagonists in world trade, energy and monetary affairs. Therefore, they are logically and basically competitors since they are competing in a world market. Where both sides, rightly or wrongly, feel threatened - as in the case of imports of Japanese cars and textiles from Third World countries - they close their ranks and present a fairly united front. Elsewhere, they simply compete with each other.

Apart from the trade war over steel which is just beginning, the other main area of contention is the Community's relations with Eastern Europe. Here, some kind of double standards may be observed. Mainly as a result of the Polish crisis, the United States is urging Common Market countries to impose stringent conditions on credit and trade deals with CMEA countries. Among the EEC countries, only the United Kingdom appears to follow the American views almost completely. However, as the West-Germans have at the Versailles meeting (held in June 1982) pointed out their own trade with the Soviet Union has declined in recent years whilst American trade with the Russians has increased! In June 1982, the United States was also negotiating a mammouth credit arrangement for the USSR to facilitate Russian purchases of American grain.

The United States has been very critical of long-term contracts made by Common Market countries with the Soviet Union for imports of Russian natural gas. The Russian deals with France and West Germany are particularly important. The author suspects that, in reality, the Americans would themselves have preferred to supply the Russians with pipelines and the Common Market countries with energy ... the business deal of the century!

However, even without the added complication of American interference, the relations between the EEC and the CMEA countries are likely to be difficult during the 1980's.

Eastern Europe

There are a number of fundamental structural reasons which make trading relations between the Common Market and the CMEA difficult. The two sides are two very different organs with completely opposite structures. The centrally planned economics of Eastern Europe (with the possible exceptions of Hungary and Yugoslavia) are not geared to world market economy prices and standards. Hence, their trading relations with the West tend to have an air of artificiality.

The Common Market, on the other hand, is a particularly well integrated group of countries with certain clear economic policies and which faces a shortage of indegenous supplies of energy and raw materials. The economic and trading policies of the EEC - where they concern agricultural and sensitive industrial products - militate against precisely those products for which CMEA countries have a comparative advantage. Thus, the only really stable and assured trading commodities which CMEA countries can export to the West are energy and raw materials. Consequently, the long-term natural gas contracts made between EEC countries and the Soviet Union are perfectly sound and logical developments - at least for the Community.

The Community's relations with Eastern Europe have been enormously complicated by the debts incurred by CMEA countries. In 1982, these debts were calculated at being approximately (gross) between 87 and 88 billion dollars. How did this state of affairs come about?

During the 1960's and the 1970's, some CMEA countries (notably Poland and Roumania) decided that the panacea for their economic development and salvation was the encouragement of industrial development. Thus, actively encouraged by the West, they set about wildly and irresponsibly importing licences and technology from the West - frequently hardly heeding the suitability of such imports to their own particular needs. In the process, the agricultural sector was frequently neglected. The results are clear for all to see. Apart from the colossal debts incurred, increased industrialisation has not proved the hoped - for panacea for their problems and some countries have been transformed from traditional food exporters into food importers.

The dramatic question which now bedevils the Community's relation with CMEA countries is what to do about these debts. Clearly, a small number of countries such as Hungary and the USSR which have good credit ratings do not present a problem. Here, problems will arise if political influences are given full play. And such influences are at work in the case of Poland. The danger is that if the Community becomes too rigid with that country over the repayment of debts, then the Poles (and that is already happening) will be forced to turn more and more to the Soviet Union and other CMEA countries for help. Furthermore, such countries can only import from the

West and pay their debts if Western countries, in turn, import goods from Eastern Europe and offer credits to these countries.

As has been seen, there is unlikely to be any problem posed by the EEC in the provision of credits and the making of positive trading arrangements where imports of energy and raw materials from CMEA countries are concerned. But trading developments between the two sides will tend to become more difficult in the 1980's if the Community does not change its agricultural policy, its attitude to imports of 'sensitive' industrial products and conditions for the giving of credits. The imposition of difficult political conditions and influences on these problems present a pessimistic picture for relations between the EEC and the CMEA in the 1980's.

Japan, China and Latin America

Perhaps the three really great challenges of the 1980's for the EEC will be Japan, China and Latin America. Japan - because it (rightly or wrongly) appears to present a threat to the Community; China - because it is a country which finds itself in the throes of great economic development and therefore offers an enormous market to the West; and Latin America - because the Common Market is at last re-discovering this important continent and suspecting that there lies a secure and reliable source of raw materials.

Although the percentage of total EEC trade with Japan is relatively small, the Community's deficit with that country continues to grow. Also, Japan has a persistent dominance (quality/price) vis-à-vis the Common Market in a number of pace-making industries (especially automobiles and electronic equipment) where the EEC should itself be competitive. Thus, the implications for the future of the Community's industrial competitiveness are extremely grave.

Relations between the two sides are further complicated by the existence of apparently non-tariff obstacles (though, in some cases, high tariffs also exist) to the entry of European goods into the Japanese market.

The immediate reaction of the EEC has been to introduce quotas for imports of Japanese goods and to make threats about the possibility of the imposition of further restrictions. Japan has made a few concessions on imports of a limited number of Community products. More constructively, the Japanese have made a number of direct investments in some EEC countries and a number of individual national enterprise in the Common Market have entered into joint ventures with Japanese companies.

Japan would seem to present a salutary challenge to the Community in the short, medium and long run. Although the imposition of quotas and the like may give the EEC a breathing space, this respite should be used to improve the Community's competitiveness.

In comparison with its contact with Japan, the Community's relations with China exhibit an aura of semi-permanent honeymoon. It should, of course, be noted that China has long desired the emergence of a strong European Economic Community and that shortly after the Chinese had recognised the EEC as a legal entity, they appointed an ambassador to Brussels (Summer 1975).

The real motor of the economic relations between the two sides is the "Four Modernisation Programmes" which were finally adopted in 1978, after fourteen years of discussion. These programmes aim at the thorough modernisation of four key sectors in the Chinese economy: agriculture, industry, national defence, and science and technology.

The over-ambitious Ten Year Plan (1976-1985) aimed at a major expansion of output in many areas - including the construction of 120 major industrial projects. Subsequently, this plan was scaled down but did not prevent an important expansion of trade between the Common Market and China. Also, an area where important future economic co-operation between the two sides may be possible is in the field of capital investment in joint enterprises. Here, after thirty years, China passed its first Joint Venture Law in 1979. This law would seem to be both flexible and generous towards foreign investors since it does allow up to a 100 per cent level of foreign ownership of companies in the country.

Trade between China and Community has tended to increase substantially since 1976 - although, even in 1979, this did not account for 0,5 per cent of Common Market trade. Thus, the EEC has taken steps to further increase its trade with China. In 1978, the conclusion of a trade agreement accorded MFN (Most Favoured Nation) treatment to both sides. This agreement has been supplemented by a Textile Agreement which came into being in 1980. This very necessary treatment does allow rather important increases in the quotas of Chinese textile exports to the Community. Equally, it places an obligation on China to supply its partner with certain raw materials used in textile manufactures - and to control the amounts of Chinese textiles exported to the Common Market. Although the actual percentage increases in the textile quotas are important when compared with the original quotas, they would have to be increased and liberalised much more substantially in future years if China is to earn the currency she needs to cover her capital and other imports in the long run.

China is also interested in exporting agricultural goods to the EEC and sees an obstacle to this development in the Community's CAP. This is a rather negative situation. Equally, it is doubtful whether China can gain much from the Community's GSP's.

The future of the Common Market's relations with China present the Community with a positive challenge. Both sides wish to see an expansion in their joint trade and China is actively encouraging Western capital investment inflows. However, the transformation of this wish into reality will depend to a large degree on changes in the EEC's own internal economic policies - as well as on the Community's ability to grant credits to China.

A different picture emerges when one turns to Latin America. Until fairly recently the Common Market (with the notable exception of West-Germany - and to some degree of France) tended to give the impression that Latin America was the Community's "forgotten continent". Indeed, considering the size and population of that continent, it is not one of the EEC's most important trading partners. The Community is, however, a major trading partner for the exports of some South American countries. Unfortunately, the exports of states such as Argentina and Uruguay have been hit by the CAP.

More recently, the Community has awoken to the fact that this continent does perhaps constitute a secure source of raw materials - one of the more permanent obsessions of the Commission. The most concrete proof of this awakening was the Community's action, this year (1982) in borrowing 600 million U.S. dollars on the international money market to lend to the Brazilian state enterprise Camanhia Vale Do Rio Doce to exploit the massive deposits of iron ore at Carajas in the Eastern part of the Amazon.

According to the author, it is perhaps Brazil, among the Latin American countries, which constitutes - in the longer term - the ideal partner for the European Economic Community. Their mutual size, development and cultural links - together with Brazil's return to democracy and that country's deep desires to loosen her ties with the United States and improve those with the Common Market - present the Community with a golden opportunity to deepen the links with Brazil by the year 2000.

Although relations between the EEC and Latin America are not easy, the contact between the Commission and the GRULA (the group of the SELA* ambassadors posted in Brussels) appear to be improving and in 1981 they examined three important areas of important specific mutual interest, energy, trade and textiles.

Finally, the area which presents the Community with the most immediate provocative and constructive challenge is the ASEAN Group of States. Initially, this group of countries with very diverse economic policy traditions and philosophies was

* The Latin American Economic System

really a defense organisation. Gradually, they have attempted to integrate their economies more closely together. Equally, they have sought greater recognition from and closer trade links with the EEC. Basically and traditionally they have supplied Western Europe with raw materials and commodities (e.g. tin, rubber, timber, and oil) in which the Europeans are not self-sufficient. More recently, they have tried to expand exports of textiles to the Common Market - a product for which they have a definite cost advantage. Naturally, this area of trade is one of conflict between the two sides. Despite this, relations between the ASEAN Group of States and the Community are in a state of active evolution and are one of the great challenges of the immediate future.

Conclusions

The European Economic Community, both in its internal economic policies as well as in its external trade relations, stands at a crossroads of critical importance. Basically, the EEC stands before the choice of 'protectionism' or a move towards the adoption of more 'open' policies. At the time of writing, the outlook is not particularly cheerful - mainly because this choice must be made against a background of international economic crisis.

The Community will almost certainly keep (and probably partially expand - if the Second Enlargement takes place) its basic more privileged trading partners such as the ACP States and the EFTA countries. But, the maintenance of constructive trade relations with other countries will depend on changes in the Community's own internal economic policies - especially the CAP - and a definite move in the direction of the adoption of an overall policy of 'product differentiation'! Such a move is more compatible with the EEC's own levels of education and technology and is the only possible option open if the Community wishes to compete effectively with such developed countries as Japan. In the very short run, it is unfortunately most likely (as demonstrated by the MFA negotiations and the new GSP's) that the temptation of protectionism will prove too strong. In the long run, however, the Common Market can only survive as the world's most important trading bloc if it energetically adopts a policy of 'product differentiation'.

Table 1 EEC Trade, by Geographical Area

	1974		1978	
	% Imports	% Exports	% Imports	% Exports
INTRA - EEC	46.86	50.58	50.00	51.57
U.S.A.	8.25	6.88	7.58	6.43
E.F.T.A.	7.44	11.25	8.91	10.89
MEDITERRANEAN BASIN	6.66	9.40	5.61	8.42
A.C.P. Countries	4.16	2.58	3.23	3.53
EASTERN EUROPEAN Countries	3.28	4.29	3.50	3.72
LATIN AMERICA	2.90	3.23	2.58	2.54
JAPAN	1.77	1.20	2.35	1.03
ASEAN Countries	0.94	1.18	1.15	1.07
REST of WORLD	17.74	9.41	15.09	10.80
TOTAL	100.00	100.00	100.00	100.00

Source: Analytical Tables of Foreign Trade, Statistical Office of the European Communities.

Table 2

Composition of EEC Trade in 1979

(in Millions of ECU's)

Description of Goods	Intra-EEC Trade	Imports from non-EEC Countries	Exports to Non-EEC Countries
Food, Beverages and Tobacco:	7.526	6.415	4.099
Minerals, Fuels, Lubricants and Related Materials:	5.987	21.254	2.459
Raw Materials:	3.090	7.762	1.390
Machinery and Transport Equipment:	17.947	9.574	19.955
Other Industrial Products (including Textiles):	30.153	19.867	22.511
Others:	1.663	4.032	3.100
Total:	66.366	68.904	53.514

Source: EUROSTAT: "Monthly External Trade Bulletin", 4/5-1981
EEC Commission, Luxemburg.

The Community's Monetary Policies

The Background: An Economic and Monetary Union

In simple terms, an economic and monetary union (henceforth referred to as EMU) is the economic, fiscal and monetary equivalent of a nation state. In more detailed terms, an EMU between countries forming a customs union or a similar arrangement replies irrevocably fixed exchange rates between the national currencies of the participating countries plus full convertibility - or a common currency. Also it implies the absolutely free movement of the factors of production (labour, capital and services), a minimum degree of fiscal integration, the co-ordination of economic, fiscal and monetary policies and the setting-up of central institutions such as a central bank. An EMU is therefore a serious and far-reaching undertaking which automatically implies a substantial degree of transfer of economic - and consequently of political sovereignty to central organs. Equally, an EMU does have a further most profound implication for participating countries. Until the final stage of the EMU, participating countries do maintain the right to use variations in their exchange rates - rightly or wrongly - in order to attempt to remedy internal economic problems - some of which may be regional in nature. Once, however, the full EMU comes into being, the same countries are no longer able to use this weapon. In fact, at this point, balance-of-payments questions between the member states cease to exist and become instead regional equilibria and disequilibria (which, of course, may have already existed in some form or other). Balance-of-payments with non-member states do, of course, continue to exist.

At the end of 1969, the EEC Heads of State agreed to move along the road towards the implementation of an EMU - to be fully achieved by 1980 - provided the "political will to do so existed". Why then, was such a momentous decision undertaken in 1969? There were, in fact, a number of reasons for this decision. Most of the aims as laid down in the Treaty of Rome

- leading to the creation of a customs union - had been achieved by 1968 - ahead of schedule. The original six EEC Member States had become highly integrated and were conducting (by 1969) about half of their trade with each other. Then, there was the Common Agricultural Policy (CAP) which really required stable exchange rates if it was to function successfully. Last, but not least, the Common Market had become the world's most important economic and trading bloc with the greatest reserves of gold and hard currencies in the West. Thus, the French considered that the Community should have a "common, international monetary personality" and that one of the best ways of achieving this would be the creation of a common EEC currency.

When, having considered a number of different plans representing different schools of thought, the Community accepted the compromise Werner Report, the ministers intended that the 'Snake in the Tunnel' should be the visible technical manifestation of the first stage of the enterprise. This Snake was the narrow band of fluctuation (of 1.2 per cent) originally planned for the central parities of the national currencies of the EEC Member States - which was to move in the wider band of fluctuation (1.5 per cent) formerly allowed for the dollar (see: diagram no.1). However, following the major dollar crisis of 1971, the suspension of dollar convertibility against gold and the subsequent Smithonian Agreement allowing a margin of fluctuation around the dollar of 4.5 per cent, the EEC had to re-examine the situation. Therefore, in March 1971, it was agreed to introduce, on an experimental basis, before 1 July 1972 (in fact this was introduced on 24 April 1972) a system whereby the margin of fluctuation around the currencies of the participating EEC Member States would be 2.25 per cent. This was to move in a dollar tunnel of 4.5 per cent (see: diagram no.2). But with the complete floating of the dollar in March 1973, the tunnel was dropped and the 'Snake' participants organised a joint float against the dollar.

The 'Snake' System did constitute a zone of monetary stability in a sea of considerable international monetary upheavals.

For most of its life it also constituted a Deutsche Mark zone - and at the close, it had become exclusively such a currency zone.

The fundamental problems which the old 'Snake' System exhibited can be ascribed to a strange combination of a lack of constraints and flexibility. Thus, because of the international monetary upheavals, some form of constraints were necessary to make inflationary levels among the participating countries converge. In turn, this implies a greater degree of co-ordination of national economic policies. On the other hand, however, the system could have been helped by more frequent, quick and probably modest adjustments in parities. Also, when one examines the problems, in the 1970's, of countries such as France, Italy and the United Kingdom, it is possible that the old 'Snake' System could have been helped by the provision of larger amounts of credits for participating countries.

During the last full year of the system's operation, in 1978, there was a growing dissatisfaction with the supposed benefits of floating. It was felt, for example, that floating was, to some degree, responsible for the upsurge of inflation. Two countries, France and West Germany, and especially their leaders Chancellor Schmidt and President Giscard d'Estaing, desired to revitalise the moves in the direction of achieving some form of economic and monetary union. The formula which was agreed upon by the EEC Member States was a European Monetary System.

The European Monetary System

The System Described

The European Monetary System (henceforth generally referred to as EMS) which came into being in March 1979, may, according to the author, be described as a de-facto monetary union. Further, should the participating countries make efforts to control inflation rates through an active co-ordination of their national economic and monetary policies, then the EMS may be seen as going beyond the first inter-

DIAGRAM No. 1

The "Snake" in the tunnel arrangement as proposed in the Werner Plan in 1970

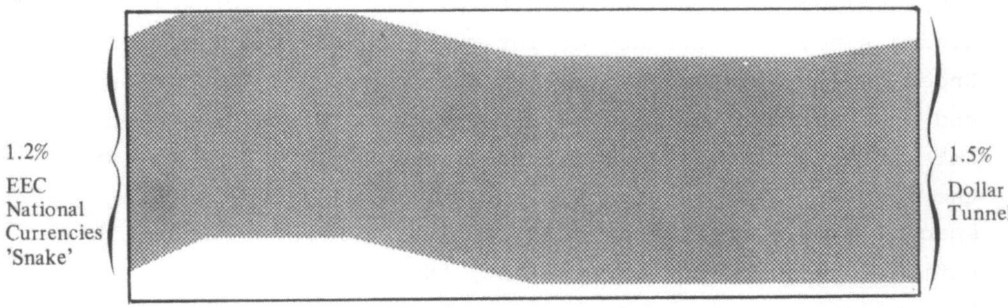

DIAGRAM No. 2

The proposed 'Snake' in the tunnel arrangement following the Smithsonion agreements in 1971

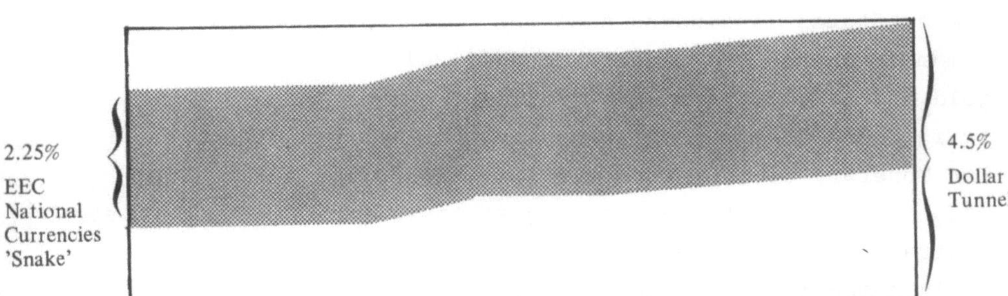

mediate stage on the road to achieving an EMU.

The EMS differs from the old 'Snake' System in a number of ways. Basically, the most important difference concerns the intervention imposed upon the monetary authorities of the participating countries. Under the old system, this was on a strict national currency to national currency basis (sometimes called a "GRID" basis) with a margin of fluctuation of 2.25%. Also, the currency of intervention was the U.S. dollar. Under the new system, intervention is both on a "Grid" basis and on a national currency vis-à-vis the ECU (the European Unit of Account) basis. Under the present "Grid" system (as the formerly) the margin of fluctuation is 2.25% - with a special margin of 6.0% allowed for Italy. However, under the national currency-ECU arrangement, the margins have been "individualised" as shown in diagrams nos.3 and 4. This 'individualisation' was necessary in order to prevent certain currencies from coming under exaggerated - and sometimes unwarrented pressures. Furthermore, there exists a "divergence" threshold - at which point, the country concerned should undertake exchange rate intervention to bring its currency into line. It is this fact that makes the EMS much more rigid than its predecessor. Under the EMS, both national EEC currencies (strongly recommended by the Commission) as well as the U.S. dollar may be used as currencies of intervention.

The EMS differs from its predecessor in many other ways. Reference has just been made to the ECU. It is intended that this unit of account should, in future, play a more active role than has hitherto been the case. Thus, the participating Member States (including also the United Kingdom which is not a member of the EMS) have exchanged 20% of their reserves of gold and U.S. dollars on a "rolling" basis. In this context, it is hoped that the existing somewhat embryonic European Fund for Monetary Co-operation will be transformed into a Fund (some even go so far as to suggest the creation of a European Central Bank) with real powers.

In comparison with the 'Snake' System, the amount of credits[5)] available to Member States - should they face

DIAGRAM No.3

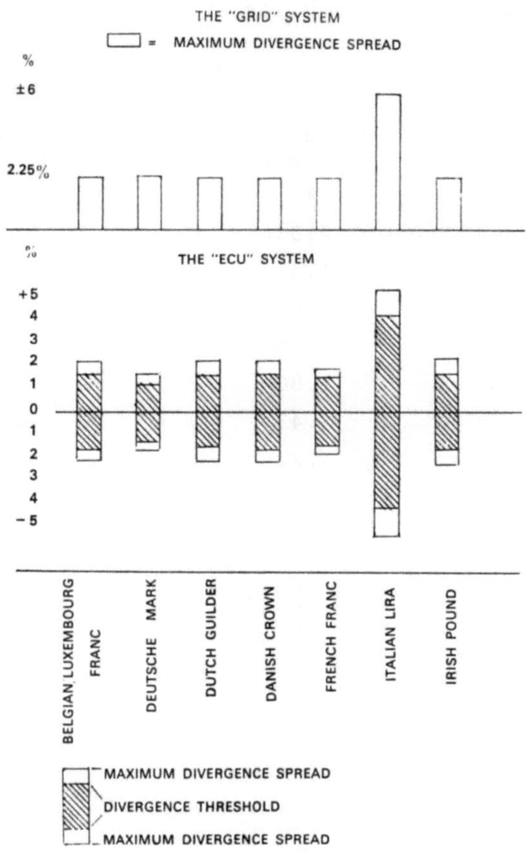

Reproduced from: "The European Monetary System - Six Months Later", P. Coffey, Three Banks Review, December 1979, London.

DIAGRAM No.4

The Commission's 'individualisation' of Maximum Divergence Spreads and Divergence Thresholds.

Currencies	Maximum Divergence Spread vis-à-vis the ECU	Divergence Threshold vis-à-vis the ECU
	%	%
Belgian/Luxembourg/Franc	2.03	1.52
Deutsche Mark	1.51	1.13
Dutch Guilder	2.01	1.51
Danish Crown	2.18	1.64
French Franc	1.80	1.35
Italian Lira	5.43	4.07
Irish Pound	2.22	1.67
Pound Sterling	-	-

pressures on their currencies and balance-of-payments problems - are substantially larger. In 1981, the approximate value of the credits (including the British contribution) was 25 billion units of account as compared with approximately 11.45 billion units of account under the former system.

A further important difference between the two systems is the degree of responsibility incumbent upon participating countries in the EMS. Thus, the Council of Ministers, in their Resolution of 5 December 1978, did clearly lay down the steps which a participating country should take whenever the Divergence Indicator is reached for its national currency vis-à-vis the ECU.

These are: "- diversified intervention,
- monetary measures,
- drawing on credit facilities, and
- external and domestic policy measures".

It is the last of these measures wherein lies the essential and only element of medium or long-term success in the future for the EMS which implies the co-ordination of national economic and monetary policies and the convergence of national levels of inflation.

<u>The System in Operation</u>

Although the EMS has not yet lead to the hoped-for convergence of rates of inflation among the participating countries, it has, nevertheless, been more successful in operation than was its predecessor. The reasons for this performance may be found in its seeming severity and flexibility. It is severe in that it causes countries to make serious attempts to bring down levels of inflation. It is flexible in that it allows swift and reasonable parity changes to take place rather discreetly. There have been a number of such changes (see: appendix 1) since the EMS came into operation.

However, a number of problems have occurred and remain. The number one problem is the relationship of the EMS with the U.S. dollar. Interestingly, one of the main reasons which encouraged the Community is to introduce the EMS was American in action in the fields of internal and external monetary policy. Now that the United States have, especially in 1981 and 1982, been taking such internal economic and monetary measures, thus strengthening the American dollar, strains have been placed upon the EMS.

More strange, perhaps, has been a totally different problem. Despite the provision of larger credits, Member States have, at times, experienced difficulties in obtaining sufficient quantities of specific national currencies of other Member States when needing them for currency intervention in the money markets. Thus, contrary to the basic recommendations embodied in the principles of the EMS, they have been forced to rely on using U.S. dollars for purposes of intervention. Also, it is interesting to note that countries are not too keen to give up their ECU's.

It had been hoped that at the ministerial meeting, held in March 1981, a decision would be taken to transform the present somewhat embryonic Fund for European Monetary Co-operation into something more substantial. However, despite the existence of a large number of plans for the creation of a more active Fund, no decision was taken about this matter.

Contrary to the afore-mentioned lack of decision and the views of many experts, the ECU has, interestingly, increased its prestige. The author had always insisted that it was mainly due to the backing of the EEC's economic and trading strength, a more attractive reserve asset than the SDR and that its main danger was the possibility of being influenced by Gresham's Law. What has in fact happened is that a number of important loans are been made in ECU's and that this unit of account may now be used for accounts in the chief centres of Belgium, France and Italy.

The Future of the EMS

As a system, the EMS faces two responsibilities. In the first case, the participating countries may finally and energetically set about co-ordinating their economic and monetary policies - and therefore making their levels of inflation converge. In which case, they will start to move quickly in the direction of achieving a real economic and monetary union.

The other possibility is the evolution of different money zones within or outside the EMS. Thus, some countries with low levels of inflation may constitute a zone of currency stability and tend to move ahead to a greater level of integration. Other countries will remain outside this zone and may or may not join or re-join it (having left it) at a later date.

Then, of course, there is the question of the Second Enlargement of the Community. Greece has already decided not to join the EMS, at least, not yet. Should Portugal and Spain join the EMS? The author would suggest that all these three countries should seriously examine the following considerations before even contemplating membership of this System.

At a strictly structural level, they should examine the amount of trade (in percentage terms of their total trade) which they conduct with the EEC. They should also critically examine their inflationary levels - both present and likely in the near future. Should they be experiencing relatively high inflation levels and balance-of-payments problems, they should calculate not only the amounts of their own reserves of gold and foreign currencies, but also possible credits - within and outside the EEC - to which they may have access. Last, but not least, they should carefully analyse their own internal financial institutional structure (e.g. banks and money markets) to ascertain whether it is adequate enough to cushion their possible membership of the EEC. In the case of Greece, apart from high Greek levels of inflation, it is also very probable that a weak internal monetary institutional infrastructure caused that country not to join the EMS.

Apart from the considerations already examined in this chapter, three major areas of development deserve particular attention for the future evolution of the EMS. These three areas are the role and future use of the ECU, moves in the direction of banking and capital market integration and the future role of the European Fund for Monetary Integration.

The Future Role of the ECU

During the nine months up to March 1982, bond issues worth 820 million ECU's had been issued. Also, in March 1982, there were approximately 12 billion SDR's in existence as compared with approximately 42 billion ECU's.

Well before the publication of these figures, the author had frequently stressed that the ECU was a more attractive asset than the SDR. In fact, the author had always warned against the possibility that the ECU might become over-attractive and become a victim to Gresham's Law. Apart (like the SDR in this one respect) from its obvious attractiveness as a spreader of risks, the ECU possesses a unique quality in its role as the unit of accounts for all the official transactions of the European Economic Community. Furthermore, its importance has been enhanced by the exchange "on a rolling basis" of the EEC Member States of 20 percent of their reserves of gold and U.S. dollars against ECU's. Thus, the viability and importance of the Community's unit of account have been well established. The question which should now be faced is what should be its future role and how should this be achieved?

There are certainly those partisans who would prefer to leave things as they are and let people and institutions themselves make their own choice regarding currencies, units of account and reserve assets. The protagonists of this school of thought would maintain that if the citizens of the EEC prefer to use U.S. dollars, Deutsche Marks, ECU's - or any other units - then they should be given the freedom to make such a choice.

At the other extreme, there are those that agree that since the ECU is the official unit of account of the Common Market, then steps should be taken to make its use as widespread as possible. Therefore, as a first step in this direction, more of the non-ECU reserves of the EEC Member States should be exchanged against ECU's. Some members of this school also suggest that national reserves thus exchanged should then become the permanent property of the New European

Fund for Monetary Co-operation.

Reference has already been made to the present position and importance of the ECU. So long as the Community exists, little or nothing is likely to change this fact because the EEC has at least to have an accounting unit for its official transactions. However, if the ECU is to become an attractive currency and/or reserve asset, it must be at least as attractive as other strong and attractive monies and assets. Also, it must be readily available to individuals and institutions wishing to hold it.

There are two ways of making the ECU's attractive: either it must carry a high rate of interest or the component currencies should be strong vis-à-vis such rival currencies as the yen, the Deutsche Mark, the Swiss Franc, the Pound Sterling and the U.S. dollar. This latter quality would seem to be best achieved by both lowering and bringing into line with each other the inflation rates of the countries whose currencies make up the ECU. The first step in this direction could be the setting of inflationary target zones.

The aim of availability should not be difficult to achieve. At the moment, only three EEC countries allow ECU's to be quoted against national currencies. Denmark has (in May 1982) expressed a lack of need to make ECU's available to its citizens since there was no demand for the Community's unit of account! Nevertheless, should citizens and institutions in the EEC wish to hold ECU's, they should be enabled to do so. Steps should be taken by the Community to bring this about.

During the present year, 1982, the launching of issues in ECU's tended to confirm the attractiveness of this asset. The tendency seems to be for this attractiveness to increase and its present success will probably engender further future successes. It is this development which will most probably increase the general use and availability of the ECU.

The Future Integration of Banking Systems and Capital Markets

Since the publication of the Segré Report, in 1966, there has been little or no progress towards developing a European

Capital Market. Segré felt that such a development would lead to (i) an increase in savings, (ii) reduce distortions in competition, (iii) lead to an optimum utilisation of funds, and (iv) help to regulate aggregate money demand through the speeding-up of necessary counter-cyclical policy.

The author, whilst not exactly agreeing with the first and fourth of Segré's criteria, would nevertheless, also list other reasons why the EEC should encourage this development. Thus, such a development would: (i) lead to a greater degree of 'transparency' in the supply of funds and therefore increase efficiency, (ii) probably help regional needs because it is likely that some Member States would insist on the creation of Community regional banks in advance or capital market integration, (iii) encourage specialisation in certain centres through the greater use of existing services and traditions, (iv) increase the Community's control of EEC borrowing on capital markets, (v) possibly diminish the necessity of EEC borrowing on non-Community markets, and (vi) facilitate the use and movement of balance-of-payments surpluses between creditor and deficit countries in the Common Market. Further, any 'real' freeing of the establishment of banking service between the EEC countries would increase the welfare of Community citizens through improved access to more and better services. This is a most important consideration which has hitherto received scant attention from economists and other specialists.

Writing over ten years ago, the author observed that the real European Capital Market was the Euro-Dollar Market for which the main centres were London, Luxembourg and Zürich. Since this observation was made, little progress has been made, and the Euro-dollar market - which is now enormous (see table below) - is still concentrated in the afore mentioned centres.

<u>Euro-Dollar Market: Approximate Value in U.S. Dollars</u>

1959: 1

1971: 78

1979:789

Although a number of directives which were passed between 1960 and 1963 did, in principle at least, liberalise the movements of capital between EEC Member States, a safeguard clause has enabled these countries to re-impose controls over such movements when the internal economic situation has justified this action. The result is that today (June 1982), the only country in the Common Market that does not impose controls over capital movements is the United Kingdom.

In the case of banking, the record is scarcely better. There have been two directives - of which only one has come into effect. This Directive (official Journal L.322, 17 December 1977) aims at the Co-ordination of Laws, Regulation and Administrative Provisions relating to the Taking-up and pursuit of credit institutions. This directive came into effect in 1980; in the case of Italy, it will be effective as from 1985. The problem with this directive is that it is too tame since it is based on the principle of equivalence.

As with capital market integration, banking developments have had little or nothing to do with official Community policy. Instead, there have been many mergers between banks in individual Member States so that the banking scene has tended to be dominated by a number of giants in each country. Any improvement in competition has tended to come from non-Community banks establishing branches inside the Common Market and through changes in national laws which have allowed banks and financial institutions to diversify the types of business which they may undertake. However, between the most important commercial banks of EEC Member States syndicates have tended to develop. This development can hardly be conductive to competition within the Common Market. So, what should be done to encourage the development of a "real" European Capital Market and to improve the establishment of banks and services between the Member States?

The experience of the past twenty years suggests that without the existence of a minimum of monetary stability it will be difficult, perhaps impossible, to move towards any real degree of capital market integration inside the European

Economic Community. Member States, facing major balance-of-payments problems, sometimes accompanied by massive capital inflows or outflows, will not easily give up the safeguards clause. Thus, the basic prerequisite is a greater co-ordination of national economic and monetary policies aimed at making national inflationary levels converge in a downwards sense. Although not yet crowned with any great degree of success, the EMS is a move in the right direction. Perhaps a greater impetus could be given to this system by the adoption of inflation targets by the countries of the Common Market.

In the meantime, however, there are a number of very minimum actions which the Community could undertake. Thus, the provision of information about capital markets for citizens in the EEC could be vastly improved. Such a move would require little effort - but it is indispensable if the EEC is serious about the creation of a European Capital Market. Similarly, the banking directive could be given some teeth. Whilst waiting for this to be done, the Commission could use articles 85 and 86 of the Treaty of Rome with a greater degree of energy where it is felt (as the author suspects in the case) that competition (and hence the welfare of Community citizens) between commercial banks should be increased.

Should nothing be done to improve matters, what is likely to happen? There is likely to be a continuation of the trends observed over the past decade. Thus, regarding capital markets we may expect centres to grow further and new centres to develop where any combination of the following conditions is fulfilled:
(i) where a country has persistent balance-of-payments surpluses, and (ii) where a centre has an established tradition of financial expertise, and (iii) where a government gives special concessions and/or specific encouragement leading to the development of a financial activity in its centre(s).

In this last context, whenever a government specifically continues to allow the Euro-dollar market to exist in its centre(s) and so long as governments, central banks, commercial banks and individuals continue to place surplus dollars on the Euro-dollar market, then one may expect this market to continue to expand - and probably in the existing centres. The one important proviso concerning the continued existence and further expansion of this market in existing European centres is the United States' decision which was implemented by the Federal Reserve Board in December 1981 whereby controls were lifted from real international Euro-currency transactions undertaken in the United States. This move is likely to have the most profound consequences for existing European centres, since, with the exception of London, no other centre can rival the expertise found in New York.

There is one last area where the Community could perhaps act as one body; this is the question of interest rates. In 1982, West Germany, the Netherlands - and to some degree Britain and Switzerland (which, of course, is not a member of the EEC) did move towards a little concertation of their interest rates. This move could be successfully further reinforced by a greater degree of co-ordination of national economic and monetary policies.

The Future European Fund for Monetary Co-operation

An embryonic Fund has in fact existed since 1973, but, the Community's credits are still managed by the Bank for International Settlements (BIS) in Basel, Switzerland, and responsibility for the management of the EMS lies with the Commission. The embryonic Fund took on more concrete potential when, with the birth of the EMS, 20 percent of the Member States' gold and dollar reserves were exchanged for ECU's. Also, reference was made to the bringing on stream of a unified European Fund for European co-operation within two years of the coming into being of the EMS. This aim did not materialise in March 1981, as was hoped, and the Community is left with a number of plans on its hands.

Criteria and Plans for a Fund

Even if the EMS does not develop much further in the foreseeable future, it would seem logical that the Community's credits should be brought under the same roof within the EEC itself rather than being managed from Switzerland - which is not even a member of the Common Market.

Further, the EMS does appear to mark a step forward in the direction of creating a full economic and monetary union. In turn, this implies a minimum degree of co-ordination of national economic and monetary policies. Here, a Fund would have an important role to play. This brings us to the question of the type of Fund which is desired. To the author there are three basic possibilities and these are as follows:

(i) a basic accounting agency where heads of EEC central banks would meet at regular intervals - a kind of Community BIS.
(ii) a form of regional International Monetary Fund (IMF), or
(iii) a kind of European Central Bank.

The first of these options could very easily and quickly be organised. The only problem facing such a development is the question of the permanent site of the Fund. In fact, the reason why the present Fund takes the embryonic form of a name-plate on a building in Luxembourg is because of the conflict of claims for its permanent home between London and Luxembourg. This problem will inevitably face any of the options adopted by the Community.

The choice of the second option, a regional IMF, would mark an important step forward in affirming the EEC's international monetary personality. Also, the question of the 'ownership' of the exchanged 20 percent of the reserves of gold and dollars of the EEC Member States need not arise. However, there would have to be some agreement about the voting power of the individual national directors on the board of managing directors.

The adoption of the third option raises the question of the

type of European Central Bank which is desirable. Basically, the choice is between the state (government) controlled central bank of the French type and the strongly independent type of central bank of the West German type. Whichever type of central bank framework finds favour, a decision to set up a European central bank would inevitably imply a high degree of economic and monetary integration.

There exists much speculation about the choice of system finding favour among the different Member States of the EEC. Conventional wisdom suggests that the British and French favour the creation of a regional type of EMF whilst the Dutch and Germans favour the creation of an independent European central bank. In fact, the West German Bundesbank has stated categorically that the setting up of a European central bank would necessitate a constitutional change and that the country would only accept a highly independent institution.

The Future of the EMS

The very success and the future development of the EMS depend upon a minimum degree of co-ordination of national economic and monetary policies among the participating countries. The aim of such co-ordination must be a convergence of inflationary levels in a downward sense.

Failure to achieve these aims will almost inevitably imply a repetition of the experience of the old 'Snake' system whereby the EEC could break up into monetary zones with a strong monetary zone moving on to a more integrated form of monetary union.

The importance of co-ordinating national economic and monetary policies is underlined by the problems associated with the disturbing influence of the US dollar, the fact that the United Kingdom is not a member of the EMS and the Second Enlargement of the EEC.

Appendix I

13. March 1979	- Introduction of the EMS.
23. September 1979	- Adjustments within the EMS (1) a 5% re-evaluation of the Deutsche Mark vis-à-vis the Danish Crown, and (2) A 2% re-evaluation of the Deutsche Mark vis-à-vis the Belgian, French and Luxembourg Francs, the Dutch Guilder, the Italian Lira and the Irish Pound.
27. November 1980	- A 5% devaluation of the Danish Crown within the EMS.
23. March 1981	- A 6% devaluation of the Italian Lira within the EMS.
4. October 1981	- A 5½% revaluation of the Deutsche Mark and the Dutch guilder. A 3½% devaluation of the French Franc and the Italian Lira within the EMS.
21. February 1982	- A 8½% devaluation of the Belgian Franc A 3½% devaluation of the Danish Crown within the EMS.
12. June 1982	- A 4.25% revaluation of the Deutsche Mark and the Dutch guilder. A 5.75% devaluation of the French Franc. A 2.75% devaluation of the Italian Lira - all within the EMS.

Notes

1. Quoted from the Introduction to "The Common Market and its International Economic Policies", Peter Coffey, NUFFIC, Den Haag, 1982.
2. The most important statement here was that made by the Commission in "The Supply with Raw Materials of the EC", Supplement of the Bulletin of the European Communities, No.1/75. This statement called for the "securing" of the Community's supplies of energy and raw materials. Since the publication of this statement, the Commission has made a number of similar calls.
3. A similar arrangement, the Arusha Agreement, was signed with three East African countries. Unlike the Yaoundé Agreements, however, this arrangement did not include the provision of financial assistance.
4. The author uses the expression "product differentiation" to mean the production by countries of goods linked with their levels of education and technological development. Thus, in the case of the EEC, the author would assume that only high quality and sophisticated goods should be produced.
5. The new credits are divided as follows: 14 billion ECU's in short-term and 11 billion ECU's in medium-term credit. A short-term credit is available for a maximum period of 9 months and a medium-term one for between 3 and 5 years.
6. The composition of the ECU, as calculated on 28 June 1974, is as follows:

0.828	Deutsche Mark	3.66	Belgian Francs
0.0885	Pound Sterling	0.14	Luxembourg Franc
1.15	French Francs	0.217	Danish Crown
109.00	Italian Lira	0.00759	Irish Pound
0.286	Dutch Guilders		

7. Thus, a Council Directive was passed on 11. May 1960 (Official Journal no.921/60, 12. July 1960), implementing article 67 of the Rome Treaty, relating to the abolition of restrictions on the freedom of intra-EEC capital movements. This Directive was supplemented and amended by a Council Directive (63/21/EEC) on 18. December, 1962 (Official Journal no.62/63 of 22. January, 1963). Unfortunately for the hoped - for freeing of capital movements, the Directive 921/60 contained a safeguard clause (article 3, paragraph 2) allowing states to maintain or reestablish controls over capital movements should a freeing of such movements jeopardise their national economic policies.

Index

MIX
Papier aus verantwortungsvollen Quellen
Paper from responsible sources
FSC® C105338

If you have any concerns about our products,
you can contact us on
ProductSafety@springernature.com

In case Publisher is established outside the EU,
the EU authorized representative is:
Springer Nature Customer Service Center GmbH
Europaplatz 3, 69115 Heidelberg, Germany

Printed by Libri Plureos GmbH
in Hamburg, Germany

OTHER BOOKS ALSO BY PETER COFFEY

"European Monetary Integration" (with John R. Presley). Macmillan, London, 1971.

"The Social Economy of France", Macmillan, London, 1973.

"The World Monetary Crisis", Macmillan, London and St. Martin's Press, New York, 1974.

"The External Economic Relations of the EEC", Macmillan, London and St. Martin's Press, New York, 1976.

"Europe and Money", Macmillan, London and St. Martin's Press, New York, 1977.

"Economic Policies of the Common Market", Macmillan, London and St. Martin's Press, New York, 1979.

"The Common Market and its International Economic Policies", Den Haag, 1983.

MAIN ECONOMIC POLICY AREAS OF THE EEC